A Graceful Passage

Notes on the Freedom
to Live or Die

ARNOLD · R · BEISSER

A Graceful Passage

DOUBLEDAY

NEW YORK LONDON TORONTO SYDNEY AUCKLAND

PUBLISHED BY DOUBLEDAY
a division of Bantam Doubleday Dell Publishing Group, Inc.
666 Fifth Avenue, New York, New York 10103

DOUBLEDAY and the portrayal of an anchor
with a dolphin are trademarks of Doubleday,
a division of Bantam Doubleday Dell
Publishing Group, Inc.

Library of Congress Cataloging-in-Publication Data

Beisser, Arnold R.
A graceful passage : notes on the freedom to live or die
by Arnold R. Beisser.—1st ed.
p. cm.
1. Death—Psychological aspects. 2. Aged—Psychology.
3. Physically handicapped—Psychology. 4. Beisser, Arnold R.
I. Title.
BF789.D4B45   1990
155.9'37—dc20   89-23367
CIP

ISBN 0-385-26766-5
Printed in the United States of America
March 1990
First Edition
BVG

To all those who have gone before, especially Dad and Stan—and all of us who will soon be joining them.

To all those individuals whose experiences I had and still have, and all those who will soon be joining them.

ACKNOWLEDGMENTS

Many people have made essential contributions to this work and I wish to acknowledge my debt to them. However, they bear no responsibility for its final form. My friends Jerry Jampolsky, Bud Blitzer, Ted Myers, Jack Levin, Jim Davy, and Marty Weinberg provided me with encouragement and advice throughout the process. Hugh and Gayle Prather were especially generous, taking time from their own busy writing schedule to help me. Dalia Blitzer carefully prepared the manuscript and Michele Biagioni helped me with the final drafts. Casey Fuetsch, my editor at Doubleday, skillfully guided the whole project to completion. Professors Norman Farberow, Robert Howell, and Carroll Kearley made helpful suggestions from their perspectives as experts in suicidology, forensic psychology and philosophy. And, of course, my wife Rita was always there to help in many different ways, some clearly identifiable and many not.

ACKNOWLEDGMENTS

CONTENTS

INTRODUCTION

TO LIVE FULLY, we cannot remain blind to the important parts of life. Even though they may be very complex and hard to face, if we do not examine them, they will return to haunt us eventually.

In this book I have tried to look squarely at an ominous part of my life that I once ignored, but that now preoccupies me. Although I have lived most of my life at death's door, in a very precarious state of health, only as I have grown older have I begun to see its implications. And I realize I must make peace with death, if I am to live my life with grace.

This is a book on the celebration of life and all its wonders. One of those wonders is death. Yet in our century it has become a taboo subject in the same way that sex was for the Victorians. Even as our population is growing older, bringing the realities of death ever closer, people seem increasingly to deny that it is an essential part of life. The realities of death need not be feared, but only what we think death is in those distorted private thoughts that interfere with living.

In urban societies only specialists deal with death, leaving the rest of us insulated and free to deny it. At the same time, we are presented with youthful images as the ideal and promised that if we use this or that product we can always remain young. And advances in the health care system are interpreted by many to mean that all disorders of the body will soon be overcome—and if not soon, at least soon enough for one to be frozen now and brought back later when they are.

Death is no more a defeat than is growing taller, starting school, or falling in love. All are phases of life, and each brings with it a special set of hazards and satisfactions. To live with grace we must be prepared to die with grace.

The question I wish to address is not whether it is morally right or wrong to consciously choose one's own death. Rather, I wish to take this issue out of the isolation in which an individual is forced by circumstances to answer for himself alone. We need not be alone even in our struggle with death. We have an obligation to each other to ease this burden that is on all of our shoulders. Whether we acknowledge it or not, death is a responsibility we share together and not something to be shunted off to hospitals and courts.

Death is as intimate and meaningful as birth, which is generally thought of as a shared experience. This does not mean, of course, that one should be denied the opportunity to die alone, but that the decisions affecting death are not a private shame or mere public policy. We must free each other in this area, and at last see that death is a part of the "right to life, liberty, and the pursuit of happiness."

I do not know how else to address this subject except through my personal experience as a doctor who has had to make life-and-death decisions and especially as a patient who often has had to face the imminence of death. My hope is that by sharing some of my most personal and intimate struggles, I can join with others who are attempting to open a healing dialogue in this area, so that, at last, birth, living, and dying can become one unified reality, a process of grace, beauty, and awareness worthy of being human.

I wish to make clear that the group considered here are people whose bodies can no longer support meaningful or fulfilling life and who have no substantial hope of improvement—the old, infirmed, severely disabled, and terminally ill. And I hope that in what I say, there is sufficient caution to anyone for whom there seems no reason for hope—that they should keep an open mind and not foreclose the future by some impulsive act.

In what follows you will see that my attitudes often shift with my health and mood, as I try to have some say in death—sometimes fearing it, sometimes welcoming or even planning for it. Many times in my life I have been convinced that everything was terminally hopeless. On each occasion thus far, this belief has turned out to be a misperception. Life actually afforded many opportunities I had been unable to see in advance. There are probably situations where no hope exists, but we cannot know this until we have looked beyond our fearful thoughts and truly experienced the situation.

Depression almost inevitably accompanies declining health and may become the great deceiver that leads to erroneous conclusions of hopelessness. It can become so isolating, that its main antidote must be communication with others. Friends, family, and professionals have often shown me aspects of reality that included hopeful opportunities that I could not see at such times.

Moreover, all perception, by its nature, is narrow and limited, creating optical illusions correctable only by time and the helpful contributions of others. Thus, no one who acts entirely alone and without giving serious attention to the views of some trusted others should ever be without some doubt.

THE GRACES

AMONG THE OLYMPIAN GODDESSES were the three Graces, who affected everything and everyone they touched with their gracious powers: compassion and good-will, refinement, and forgiving gentleness. As the most powerful of gods, Zeus and the favored Apollo kept the Graces with them whenever they could.

Only sullen Pluto, the ruler of death and the dead, scrupulously avoided the Graces, fearing that the consistent grimness of his domain might be compromised by their joy and brilliance and bloom. These were, in fact, their names: Euphrosyne for joy, Aglaia for brilliance, and Thalia for bloom.

One fine summer day Zeus, as ruler of all the gods and goddesses, ordered them all to assemble. Looking for a little fun, he arranged for the dour Pluto to sit next to the Graces fair. With aloof resolve, Pluto barely seemed to notice them, and when he did, he showed disdain. However, the Graces, always generous and forgiving, showed only compassion and goodwill. And soon, their charms proved irresistible even to him, the master of darkness and gloom.

Embarrassed by his failed determination, he hurried home. Yet even as he crossed the river Styx, the influence of the three stayed with him: from Aglaia came light to balance darkness, from Thalia's bloom, an equilibrium to rival the gloom, and from the lovely Euphrosyne, there was joy to match the doom.

The next time Zeus summoned Pluto to his court, he was shocked to see his countenance had changed—absent was his familiar woeful desolation. Alarmed by what he saw, the often stern Zeus asked, with much concern, "What did the Graces move you to, my friend? I saw you part from them."

Pluto smiled benevolently and said, "They moved me, yes, but not as you might think. They felt sorrow that I left. So, their gentle influences followed me to my dominion, showing me that I have no corner on darkness or gloom, nor they on joy and light. So now I know, I am no different from the other gods, nor they from me. Like the mortals, what we make of life and death is what we think they are."

A Graceful Passage

ONE

Hazards of Immortality

DEATH SPEAKS:

There was a merchant in Bagdad who sent his servant to market to buy provisions, and in a little while the servant came back, white and trembling, and said, "Master, just now when I was in the marketplace, I was jostled by a woman in the crowd, and when I turned I saw it was Death that jostled me. She looked at me and made a threatening gesture; now, lend me your horse, and I will ride away from this city and avoid my fate. I will go to Samarra, and there Death will not find me." The merchant lent him his horse, and the servant mounted it, and he dug his spurs in its flanks and as fast as the horse could gallop he went. Then the merchant went down to the marketplace and he saw me standing in the crowd and he came to me and said, "Why did you make a threatening gesture to my servant when you saw him this morning?" "That was not a threatening gesture," I said, "it was only a start of surprise. I was astonished to see him in Bagdad, for I had an appointment with him tonight in Samarra."

JOHN O'HARA, *Appointment in Samarra*

WHEN I WAS GROWING UP, death was no more than a midnight whisper. I never knew my grandparents—I never saw a picture of even one of them. They died thousands of miles away before I was born. They could also just as easily have been dead for a thousand years, for all I knew.

My father did not even know his parents, for they died shortly after he was born. And I knew only a little about my mother's. They died in Europe when she was still in her early teens—far away and long ago to me.

My mother and father both came to America as young teenagers, eager to forget the hardships and persecutions of their native Russia, and ready to embrace this new land completely. They wanted to leave the past behind them, and there was so much they wanted to become.

The opportunities in this glistening new land seemed to erase generations of hardship from their minds. They quickly became indistinguishable from native-born Americans, and learned to speak English without a trace of an accent. My brother and I knew little from their backgrounds, for there was not much they wanted us to preserve. We learned to look ahead.

It was as if my dead family members had never lived and life had only begun with my parents, my brother, and me. No one from my immediate family had ever died during my lifetime so, as a reality, death simply did not exist for me. It certainly held no terror.

My childhood legacy was one of long silence—except at midnight.

In the quiet darkness, something infinite would appear. It was nothing and yet everything, a stranger to my world of action and light. I was not afraid of it, for I had no reason to be. So I willingly entered its murky depths, there to travel among mysteriously appealing images from unknown origins. They were oddly broken forms without labels that became my friendly introduction to the peaceful silence of the bygone.

But I knew the mystery in another form as well—when the adult voices dropped and there were whispers from another room. "Never mind" was its first name. It became an ominous, yet compelling, invitation to try to comprehend that ineffable place.

It was many years more before the name "death" entered my private unearthly darkness. Then familiar ghostly forms of dead schoolmates would appear in the stillness of the night—Lucille and Lyle and Galen were their names.

Each had disappeared from life in much the same way, although at different times. All one day, their school desks remained unoccupied, like newly placed tombstones, inviting our furtive glances. We waited, but they never appeared in class again. We seemed to know what had happened to them, so our teachers must have told us, but all I remember was the hushed silence coming from their vacant seats.

That was all I knew of death until I was nineteen, when my father died. Once he was powerfully built, but as his illness grew, I watched him gradually shrink to half his size. This agonizingly slow decline lasted nearly half my life, almost a decade. My brother and I were partly insulated from his suffering during the last few years of his life, when we were away from home in World War II military service or in college.

It was my mother who carried the heaviest burden. She faithfully nursed him to the end, helpless to stem the erosion of his health and the family assets, no matter how hard she tried. For a time she even tried to continue to operate the family bicycle store, until she had to devote all her strength to trying to keep my father comfortable.

In the midst of World War II, mortal struggles were winding down everywhere, it seemed. When my father's end did finally come, my brother, having been through the worst of the fighting in Europe, was granted leave to return home for the funeral. I was stationed only a few hundred miles away in a Navy school, and I too got leave to come home.

Although I missed my father terribly, knowing that his suffering was at an end made his death as much relief as sorrow for us. I also felt as though his death had lifted a heavy weight from my back. Even the feeling of injustice that I had felt about his suffering, and the burden it had been for my mother, began to dissipate.

Moreover, since this was the first time in years that the rest of our small family—my mother, my brother, and I— were at home together, it seemed more like a celebration than a funeral. My brother's life had been in grave jeopardy throughout the war, and now here he was home intact. I remember feeling guilty that this sad occasion seemed so joyful. But I did feel happy.

However, my feelings were more complex than I realized, and I did not know their depth until one of the most inexplicable acts of my life occurred when I returned to naval school. I was far behind in my work, and had to catch up.

I sequestered myself to study, but one of my fellow Navy students, well known for the pleasure he derived from taunting others, refused to leave me alone to work. He stood around talking to me and making sure I could not study. I asked him several times to leave me, each time in stronger terms. That only seemed to stimulate him to harass me more.

Then it happened. I exploded! I attacked him in mindless fury. I was oblivious to what might happen, and I am afraid I might not have stopped at all except that the commotion brought others to the scene, friends who restrained and calmed me.

Fortunately for both of us, he was not hurt badly. I was probably as shaken as he was, for I had never been so completely out of control before. It was a part of me I had never seen before and did not know at all. Where had that pent-up fury come from?

What I did know was that it happened immediately after my father's funeral. There I felt a lot of undifferentiated anger, but with no one I could blame. My father's senseless suffering, my mother's near-saintly self-sacrificing loyalty, my own inability to be of help, my brother's being away, and then, just as senseless, there was relief, along with the loss of the father I loved. My hapless tormentor made himself a perfect target for it all. "Rage, rage against the dying of the light."

Thus it was that death entered my daylight hours as well as my midnight reveries. I now knew it by name and in unadulterated form—senseless, tormenting, absolute, far-reaching, brutal, and inevitable.

Death is innately senseless and absolute. It is certainly inevitable, but does it have to be as brutal and tormenting as my father's was? That it was so prolonged and eroding, scarring a whole family, was not absolute or inevitable. Those were not qualities of death itself, but of the very human pathway to it.

Would my father have preferred to shorten its course? To get it over with, at last? I do not know, and I doubt he knew it as an option. I know my mother loved him deeply, and saw no other way for herself but sacrifice. Was there ever any part of her that would have preferred that it be over?

What about my brother? He is no longer here for me to

ask. Was it only I who wished my father's agony to be done with in some humane form? Perhaps I was only self-serving, wanting him dead for my own relief?

I do not know. What I do remember was wanting desperately for his pain to stop. I remember wanting him to be stronger, like the father I knew first. I wanted him to tell me what to do, instead of the other way around, with my taking care of him. I remember envying those whose fathers were strong and healthy.

So I was not afraid of death. It was nothing more than my friendly after-midnight darkness, filled with unexpected forms. But what I learned from watching my father was that the road to death can also lead to the erosion of the life that does remain, and that is what I feared—pain and suffering, the agony of survivors, and the erosion of fond memory.

As a medical student and then a doctor, I found death a constant enemy. I spent my time trying to outmaneuver it, in what was quite literally mortal combat. When death won, I thought I failed; when the patient survived, I thought I won. It was the same kind of competition on which I thrived in sports.

Although my fights with death were for my patients' sake and, I thought, solely in their own behalf, when death was in retreat, I seemed to think that I had won. As far as my personal health was concerned, I behaved as if I were immune to death. I was strong and athletic and had not yet been threatened by death, so what did I have to fear? I had not joined the human race.

Sometimes I would pause to look upon the face of death, a patient that just had turned to a corpse, and wonder about it all. I would soberly try to fathom its mystery. What did it mean? What could it mean? I know I was in awe. But still there was no terror; it was only like my after-midnight friend.

A few days after I turned twenty-five, all that changed. To my great surprise I joined the human race—I discovered I was vulnerable just like everyone else. I became deathly sick with polio and completely paralyzed, kept barely alive by an iron lung. I did not want to die, it was not supposed to be my time, some gross mistake must have taken place, I thought.

Something was seriously wrong. Someone got the roles all mixed up—I was the doctor, not the patient; I was the physically strong one who helped others. I had work to do; I could not be sick. I did not have the time. Like millions before me, I thought, "I am too young to die."

But even as I fought with death on my own behalf, it did not seem real, but once removed. In my delirium I saw not death, but a test in school. For this particular test I was totally unprepared. I had not been to class, and was not even sure what its subject was. Yet here I was, and I had to take it unprepared. If I flunked, my career would be ruined. That seemed a fate equivalent to death.

I lingered on, in terror, half alive, for weeks and weeks and weeks, struggling to awaken from the nightmare's grasp. Yet, each time I caught a glimpse of how I actually was in life, without the ability to move or breathe, I shrunk back in fear into my nightmare. I was caught between the delirium of flunking out of school and the living horror of complete paralysis, uncertain which ordeal was worse.

And so I learned the fear of death, or at least that is what I thought it was. I did not know whether I passed or failed the test; I guess I barely passed, because I was alive. But I nearly flunked, for in the years that followed, both my paralysis and my fear of death remained unchanged.

I thought my fear of death was justified. Because my hold on life was tenuous and could be interrupted by even a common cold, I was simply being realistic, I thought. So I lived cautiously, and took no chances, always fearing that I might take on too much for me to manage. I lived in continuous fear that I might die. What I did not know was that I had become limited as much by my fear and caution as by paralysis.

If others knew, they did not say. Using disability as a rationalization must have been too much for them as well. It can be such an impenetrable shield. It took a loyal friend and teacher to show me what it was. Then I could see that my fear of death was no more or less than a fear of life, a means of avoiding even the small risks that give the feel of life to emptiness.

"I cannot live because—" is a sad betrayal of life's opportunities. Death is the unknown, and to fear the unknown, whatever it may be, is only to fear what you have already learned from life. To base what you do now entirely on what you learned from last year's encounter makes any change impossible. If you live in safety at the price of feeling dead, you will have chosen monotony over opportunity.

That is what immortality would be, life without risk or fear. It would feel like death. You could never take a chance, because you could do the same thing again and again endlessly, until you got it right. But it really would not matter. There could be no failures, so no successes either. Without death, life would have no worth or meaning.

Thus the polarity to life is not death; it is immortality. To live completely, to go "all the way" with life, requires holding *nothing* back—accepting that this *is* life, and by its very definition, it means that we must die.

We say that people die of heart disease, or accidents, or poor nutrition, or even malpractice. People even sue for "wrongful death." But those are not the major causes of death; they are merely incidental or precipitating events. The cause of death is life! You cannot have one without the other.

Still, immortality is the false aspiration cherished by mortals. To try to live forever, people visit doctors regularly, jog many tortured miles, eat tasteless fat-free, salt-free food, quaff down tons of vitamins, and submit to dreadful operations. If those should fail, they can always have themselves frozen cryogenically. Anything will do, as long as it might keep them alive.

Some seek immortality in other ways. They have lots of kids, build stone monuments and financial empires. And since words and stories can outlast the earthly presence of those from whom they came, they write long books or covet fame. Some believe they will continue to live after they die—only in some other place, where their virtue will be rewarded and their evil punished. Some believe they do not die, but return in other earthly forms.

Each of these beliefs can serve people well, and indeed may well be true. For they are articles of faith, and not subjects for the experimental method and scientific investigation. However, they can also be used as a vain attempt to avoid the inevitable truth of life and death as well. They can be used to avoid responsibility for our every act as we defer until that "better day." But, just as "the proof of the pudding is in the eating," the proof of life is in the living —and the dying.

The footprint is not the foot, and what lives after death is not life as we know it now. To live this life fully requires that we accept the truth of its inseparable companion, death. So if we celebrate one, why not the other? To cherish one and deny or fear the other is to artificially divide truth, and discard half of it.

So, here's to life . . . and death as well!

TWO

A Matter of Life and Death

To be, or not to be, that is the question:
Whether 'tis nobler in the mind to suffer
The slings and arrows of outrageous fortune,
Or to take arms against a sea of troubles
And by opposing end them. To die—to sleep,
No more . . .

SHAKESPEARE, *Hamlet*

IN A FEW MONTHS I will have reached sixty-four years of age, hardly to be considered a major accomplishment under ordinary circumstances. However, I have not lived most of my life under ordinary circumstances, and no betting man would have placed a wager on my still being here if he knew the odds. Of course that's what insurance actuarials do, and I have not been able to get any insurance in the open market for nearly forty years. The bets were clear that I wouldn't make it.

I've been on life-support systems nearly all that time. I spend half of the twenty-four-hour day in an iron lung, a gargantuan leftover from the days before the Salk and Sabin vaccines eliminated polio. During the other half of the day I intermittently must use other kinds of respiratory support machines.

But breathing has not been my most serious difficulty. That has been being unable to move by myself. The only muscles that I can work are in my face, in part of my neck, and a little bit in my right hand. Beyond that I am completely paralyzed.

When I'm not in the iron lung and when I'm not lying in bed I have an electric wheelchair that compensates for a great deal by doing magical things. With a few micro-switches I can drive about, and I can elevate my legs and recline the back so that I am lying entirely flat—the position in which I am most comfortable.

There aren't very many of us old polios left ("poliaks," as one of my fellow casualties calls us) and I've watched my friends who were disabled as severely as I am gradually die off. Of the few "old poliaks" still left, most were not as completely affected as I am.

I realize more and more that just how disabled someone is cannot easily be defined. It cannot be based solely on a doctor's judgment, or on how much physical incapacity someone has. It has more to do with what it's like for a person subjectively. And how disabled someone feels depends on what the person believes himself to be and what he believes he should be, that is, whatever gives meaning to his life.

A boy soprano whose voice has changed may be more disabled than a mathematician who loses the use of his legs; a twisted ankle may be worse for a ballerina than paralysis for a stockbroker; and a business tycoon may never recover from the loss of his secretary.

Insofar as you consider something an essential part of who you are, all losses can hurt equally. Losing a leg is a lot like losing someone you love, your job, your car, or even your belief in the Yankees.

I have had to revise who I thought I was many times, in

order to make life bearable. Each time, it was very hard, for I had to give up thinking of myself in a particular way that seemed important and valuable.

However, that is what you *have* to do in order to survive and find any peace at all. You have to be able to discover interests in the world you currently live in, not just in the one that used to be.

Of course there are alternatives. You can refuse to give up your old ways and insist there is nothing new out there for you. You can escape into fantasy and make believe things have not changed from what they were. But unfortunately those are usually only temporary solutions and reality does have a way of catching up with you. Then you have to die or accept one of the forms of living death. You cannot live in the past or just deny the whole affair for very long.

During the stock market crash of '29, suicide was chosen by some who could not live without their money. A person whose life is work may retire, and then collapse. A child may refuse to start going to school, unable to bear leaving home and mother. An athlete may not accept that his career is over, and fall into sadness and despair.

For years I would read the obituaries in the various medical publications to which I subscribe with a puzzling mix of emotions. When I would see the name of someone I knew, I had a momentary sense of triumph that I had outlasted someone who seemed stronger than I. Of course, that was mixed with sadness over the loss of the colleague and friend and I felt guilty about feeling triumphant, for my hapless colleague had done nothing wrong.

But then, I really did not expect to live this long. Most of the time, I did not think about life or death very much, for I was too busy just getting along day to day. Now, somewhat to my amazement, here I am, still.

Many times during these years I thought I might die—when I would get a cold, for example, since I cannot cough or sneeze or blow my nose; for even minor ailments can be life threatening for me. Sometimes it was not even related to my own ailments. Each year on the anniversary of my older brother's death, now some eight years past, I began to think I would die. But as I said, here I am.

Now, however, it does seem like I am not going to be able to hold out much longer, and when my life becomes too physically burdensome, I really don't want to. Aside from the general decline caused by the aging process, I have acquired a whole catalog of more recent unpleasant physical problems.

My breathing is worse now, of course, but among the new things are that my legs, which have been of no positive use to me for forty years, now are a source of great discomfort. They usually feel as if they are on fire and I should cool them off. However, to the touch they are cold. The years of inactivity and diminished circulation have taken their toll.

My back gives out whenever it is jarred and it has become so demineralized from years of lying flat that any unusual movement produces pain. Then I am forced to lie immobilized in bed again, sometimes for weeks on end.

Abdominal pain attacks that have sent me to hospital emergency rooms recently are assumed to be of liver and/or gallbladder origin. In fact, now that I think about it, almost every organ of my body is defective in some way. Fortunately things like hypertension and skin cancer, my growing prostate problems, and most of the dermatoses from which I suffer aren't as unpleasant.

But you know what the worst thing is? I now have to spend almost half of my time when I am outside my iron lung dealing with bowel care problems, leaving precious little time for more interesting matters. Those problems make me quite uncomfortable much of the rest of the time. That I am willing to write about such an indelicate and taboo subject is the real evidence of how far my decline has gone. "Pride goeth . . . before a fall."

I have described a pretty grim picture, haven't I? And by now I probably have lost most of you, because there is nothing more boring than someone telling you about his bad health. In fact, there is nothing more boring *to me* than thinking or talking about my own ill health. And indeed the whole matter would be simplified if what I have described were all that made up my life.

But in addition, I have my moments. Moments when I am in contact with whom and what I love—my friends, my work, my wife, my mother, and the patients I still see in my psychiatric practice, although sadly for me that has become a diminishingly small part of my week's activities.

I am working on a new book, and I am enjoying the NBA basketball play-offs.

But now, it seems, too much of my time is spent sitting in doctors' offices, undergoing various tests, going to hospital emergency rooms when I am in acute distress, and doing other things that are not rewarding at all. I don't really even want to think about how little of my time is left to spend in other activities. If I did, it would be too frightening.

One of the worst aspects is witnessing the effects of my decline on those I love and who love me. I see the pain that my decline causes them. Their desire to help me is touching, but when they cannot, they feel bad. I hate causing them discomfort as much as I hate having it. I realize how burdensome I have become to others, as well as myself. If I cannot be of help to others and they cannot help me, there is not too much left.

I have always been afraid of being a burden to others and it's always been extremely difficult for me to ask for and seek out what I need for myself alone. To be assertive for others or for a cause is easy, but on my own behalf, I am afraid I am a failure.

My family was very close when I was growing up. We all helped one another, and knew that others were there for us. We worked together in the family bicycle store. We felt deserving, because we could be helpful to each other and were. I was expected to do my part, like everyone else, and when I did I felt worthwhile. But I also grew up feeling that only when I was useful, was I deserving. And now, as my capacity to do things for others, or to accomplish anything at all, diminishes, so too does my sense of self-worth.

I sometimes entertain what for me is the ultimate horror story—being in a hospital where the health care system has taken over my life and moves inexorably toward decisions about me in which I would have little or no say. That seems very grim indeed, helplessly being kept technically alive without choice.

My breathing problems would almost certainly require that I be intubated or given a tracheotomy and that would make me unable to speak or to protest against anything that might be done to me. This combined with my physical inability to move or signal in some other way would render me unable to communicate at all, utterly and completely helpless, without even a modicum of control over my life.

When I first became disabled I found the hospitalization experience painfully humiliating beyond description. So my main goal became finding ways of regaining some control over my life. Eventually, through good fortune, the help of others, and considerable effort, I did manage to reach this goal in part. It necessarily had to be a different kind of control, for I never regained the ability of voluntary movement. Now what is most frightening to me is contemplating the loss of even that symbolic control.

I know that I am not alone in this dread of helplessness and loss of control. In a National Institute of Mental Health report concerning survivors of terrorism, prison camps, and concentration camps, a major finding related to control. All of the people studied had the authority for their own lives torn away from them.

A characteristic common to those who survived, and did so without being emotionally crushed or mentally devastated, was that they found some symbolic way of retaining some control of their lives. For example, one captive found that by treating his captors as though they were guests when they entered his cell, he added a voluntary element to his captivity. This helped him to maintain a sense that he was not completely helpless. Even if it was mainly an illusion, it helped him maintain his sanity.

So I want to take steps to assure myself that I will not lose the last vestige of control. I have my "living will" in front of me, and I have the durable power of attorney which I will give to my wife, for she knows what my wishes are. But as a doctor, I know that may not be enough.

The medical solutions to the problems with my legs, my gallbladder, and my urinary tract are all surgical. Surgery requires anesthesia, and in my case the very least requirement for sound anesthesiology practice would be intubation, and that is when the scenario I dread would begin. A tube in my windpipe would make virtually any form of communication impossible for me. That is when the forces which control a hospital patient's destiny automatically begin to work their will.

Committed as they are to saving lives, hospitals, doctors, and nurses are caught between the twin legal pressures from malpractice insurance on the one hand and "right to life" legislation on the other. The system keeps people alive, whatever the quality of their lives, whatever the quality of discomfort they feel or what their wishes are.

The advocates who place the health care system and its doctors and nurses in these binds are well meaning, for who would argue against the sanctity of life and the right to live? And who could argue against holding doctors accountable for their mistakes? However, what their activities have now produced is inertia and fear.

The militant ideologues who insist one way alone is correct do not have to stay around to witness the unnecessary human suffering and the tragedy of spent lives maintained beyond use or meaning. They advocate conflicting ideas that make the system ponderous and inflexible. They unwittingly sacrifice a person in despair on the altar of a "good" idea.

They counter by insisting that modern means of pain control will fend off whatever problems there are. But I am enough of a physician to know just what those pain control effects are and I have experienced them firsthand as a patient as well. They are not so innocuous or as relieving as their advocates assure us. If given for any length of time, they all have their own ways of contributing to patient discomfort and misery.

Moreover, I am, as the expression goes, a very poor "surgical candidate," and the chances of my surviving after surgery are much diminished. The extent of surgery that could be performed on me would only be palliative at best and produce only brief results. So why should I go through the agony when the odds are stacked against me anyhow? I've decided that I do not wish to place myself in that jeopardy.

Nothing is easy, but dying is especially difficult, if you choose to have any control in the matter. I could probably stop using my life-support respirators at home; however, it might take weeks before I would die and it could be prolonged agony for me and everyone around me.

If I were to try to accelerate the process, I would need help, and I would hate to place that burden on someone else. So I would have to figure out a way of doing it without involving others in the task.

I'm really sorry about that, because I'd like to be open and honest with my friends and family. In fact, I'd like them to be with me for support if they did not mind.

I've had fantasies of inviting a whole group of friends to what would be a "celebration of choice," celebrating that I had been able to live and die as I wished. I would envision a partylike atmosphere, perhaps much the same way that I imagine it was for Socrates when, surrounded by his students, he drank the hemlock.

When I think about this, what stops me is those who will remain after I am gone. I would not want to place the people I care about in legal jeopardy, but I have other, more private concerns too. The people whom I love also love me, and at the very least they would experience a sense of loss.

I know also that my relationships are based on interdependence, and there would be a certain loss of purposeful-ness without me. But most of all, because they are the kind of caring people that they are, my loved ones might feel responsible in some way, and think perhaps that they should have done more. But nothing could be further from the truth. They have done all they could and more. The greatest gift that could be given to me now, or to anyone, would be to allow me to live and die on my own terms.

When a loved one dies, the survivors may have prob-lems if they are unprepared or if the event has some hidden elements. They are likely to feel guilty or ashamed, and blame themselves. If the whole experience is open, honest, and aboveboard, they may feel that at least they have acted responsibly. Then the loss will heal in time. That is why I hate subterfuge.

Timing presents another problem, for if I were to wait too long, I might not be able to carry out my wishes. The health care system might already have begun to grind, and I would become its pawn again. And, of course, I have no desire to end my life, except as a way of avoiding useless suffering, so as long as there is hope, I would like to stay. So timing is critical.

Is trying to exercise control in the matter of my own death asking more than as a mortal I should dare to have? Is all of this obsession about my own death just a spurious attempt to assume godlike omnipotence? I must and do accept that I have no control over what the forces of na-ture may bring at any time.

However, this is not an issue between me and God, but

between me and what man has created. Health care services are made by men and men can err. Good things can be used for purposes that make them bad sometimes.

Without the health care system, I would have died nearly forty years ago. I am glad I did not. I am glad the health care system was there to keep me alive, for at that time my future was before me and my life has been rich. I have no regrets.

But now most of my years are behind me, and although I hope I have more time because there are things to do, I hope when it is time to go I can exit gracefully.

I hope I am not kept artificially alive when unable to do anything of worth. That would be beyond faith or reason, and I have seen how degrading and humiliating senseless health care intervention can be. I have seen the erosion of the spirit that can occur when people become caught up in the gears of that well-intentioned machine.

Aesculapius was the Greek god of medicine and the forerunner of modern medicine. He became so skilled at keeping people alive that no one died. This threatened Pluto as the undisputed ruler of the underworld and the dead. His domain was becoming underpopulated because so many people were kept alive by Aesculapius' medical skills. The balance between the living and the dead was becoming disturbed.

Pluto complained to Zeus, the king of the gods, that his kingdom was being deprived. Zeus, after careful thought, concurred; he perceived grave danger that so many who should have died, instead survived. At last he intervened to restore the precarious equilibrium, and, to compensate Pluto, he sentenced Aesculapius himself to the underworld of the dead.

I have been cheating Pluto for almost forty years with the aid of skillful ministrations by physicians—the contemporary descendants of the Aesculapian tradition. Have I disturbed a sacred balance by living this long? To this point, I feel I can justify my life by what I do and have done. But what about when that usefulness is gone and there is nothing more that I can do?

I know that Pluto will have his way in the end, he always does. However, is it possible to live too long? The questions that remain in my case are, Who will make the decision that my time has come and when? Shall I rely on Zeus or some successor god to intervene when the time is right? Can I trust the wisdom of the current Aesculapian system to know when its job is done? Or should I rely on me, at least in part?

THREE

Dying Without Wings

In the neighborhood there was a famous dervish who was considered the best philosopher in Turkey; Candide, Martin, and Pangloss went to consult him. Pangloss was the spokesman, and said to him: "Master, we have come to ask you to tell why such a strange animal as man was ever created."

"What are you meddling in?" said the dervish. "Is that your business?"

"But, Reverend Father," said Candide, "there is a horrible amount of evil on earth."

"What does it matter," said the dervish, "whether there

is evil or good? When His Highness sends a ship to Egypt, is he bothered about whether the mice on board are comfortable or not?"

"Then what should we do?" said Pangloss.

"Hold your tongue," said the dervish.

"I flattered myself," said Pangloss, "that you and I would reason a bit together about effects and causes, the best of all possible worlds, the origin of evil, the nature of the soul, and pre-established harmony." At these words the dervish shut the door in their faces.

VOLTAIRE, *Candide*

T HE INVENTIVE GENIUS of mankind has been most clearly manifested in its capacity to live without truly living, and to die without really dying. That is what makes it possible for people to go through *life* as though they were dead, oblivious to its natural wonder; then they can insist that when they die, they will not really be dead.

We sometimes look at the world as nothing more than something to be used, a commodity that has its only value in monetary terms. The only purpose of it as far as we can see is exploitation—today. We want either to own the world or to have it entertain us.

At other times we may behave as if life is something "to get through" and endure. That leaves us unable to respond with interest and enthusiasm to the opportunities before us; we ignore the awesome power of the universe that surrounds us, unwilling to examine the meaning of it all. We can go through life and know little of our own capacity for love, reverence, imagination, and responsibility.

We may rarely think of the meaning of existence, but

when we do, it may seem so empty that we cannot believe that that is all there is. So we insist that death is not death at all. We insist we will not die, but will just live a better life in heaven, where all our hopes will be fulfilled. Or we think we will return to earth in different forms again and again, until our lives reach perfection.

How many people do you know who look upon each day with eagerness and anticipation? Not many, I will wager. We often live in dull routines, one day just like the next. Nothing new or unexpected is exciting enough. Nothing familiar looks safe enough. We shrink from things of abiding value that are stimulating, fearful that if we become too involved, we might have to suffer painful loss. Perverting the ancient wisdom, our banner sometimes seems to read, "it is better not to have *ever* loved, than to have to face the danger of a loss."

The great curse of modern life is that we may awaken each morning in fear of what is to come, instead of welcoming it as a friend; we can look out upon the wonders of the dawn and see only a forbidding night ahead, or even worse, nothing at all. To ignore the possibilities in the present, to reject the earthly wonders as they are—that is man's genius gone mad.

Then, to compensate for that lack of joy and meaning in life, we put off the prospect of fulfillment until we are dead. We say we will have our chance to live—in another life on earth through reincarnation, or in a better place than earth, such as eternal heaven.

I do not deny that these are possibilities; I simply do not

know, and will not know while I am on this earth. No one who has gone before has come back to tell us. But my objection is not to what may come in the future, whatever it may be. Not at all. Rather, it is the way in which the "yet to come" is used to repudiate the opportunities that are already here.

Some of us want a second chance at life, when we have not used the first. We want immortality, life that is forever, when we do not live this day fully. To be afraid of death is but to fear what is unknown in life—to be afraid of living. And that is where the problem rests.

Is the ideal life we seek devoid of loss, disappointment, and pain? Do we expect to have nothing but success, good health, and love? If so, it never happens that way. And since we know it won't, is it possible to feel alive when we cannot be as we want, do as we want, or fulfill our fondest dreams?

My dreams were crushed when I was still quite young. I lost what I loved most: I could not be the person I once was, and could not become the one I planned to be. For I have spent more than half of my life completely paralyzed and unable to live the way people are supposed to live. I lost my profession, my recreation, many friends and loved ones, my ability to move and even breathe.

The title of my previous book, *Flying Without Wings,* is a metaphor to describe my quest to find my way when all seemed lost. This was largely a description of my personal odyssey in living with my disability; however, the problems of dealing with loss, pain, and the imminence of death are common to all people and, along with discovering what there is to affirm in life, comprise *the* issues of living well.

I have facetiously called this chapter "Dying Without Wings," partly to make fun of the metaphor in my previous book. Not taking myself too seriously has been important to me in surviving adversity and in coming to terms with my disability.

Also, the phrase "dying without wings" points out a compelling paradox. It is impossible to seriously consider life without recognizing the importance of its opposite, death. To live well, you must come to terms with death, and to die with grace you must have come to terms with life.

If wings of fantasy must be fabricated in order to face life and death, their reality still remains unmet. Moreover, it *is* possible to live and die with the same passion we associate with flying, and without fooling ourselves. To really fly, you have to use real wings that you can touch and see and feel, not ones of "make believe." But to do so requires that you trust what you know to be true.

What I can touch and see and feel may not be the same for you, but common to all of us is a capacity to be true to ourselves. And I have experienced wondrous moments, moments of exalted peace within, and not only when all was going well. Perhaps the heaven usually sought in some future time and place may be found right here, if we can find the way to see it now. And if that is true, why wait until we die to have it in another place, if we can have it here? The process of meeting each moment squarely is critical, and the opportunity is there for rich and poor, crippled and able-bodied, black and white, people of every belief.

If life is a journey, then everyone has death as a hidden traveling companion. Usually unseen and, as a rule, unwelcome, it can appear without notice at any time to torment or offer solace. When illness struck me down, death emerged from hiding and has remained with me ever since, never far from center stage.

It has appeared in different forms depending on how much pain, disability, and anguish I have felt. Sometimes it has been a threatening executioner that terrified me, at other times it was an appealing Siren's call beckoning me away. But always it has remained a persistent teacher, reminding me that this *is* life, and it could be over at any moment.

Death showed me that I had better learn to live right now—there may not be another sunset, another opportunity for love, or another time for this particular encounter with joy, agony, gain, loss, peace, or pain.

Unfortunately, it has not been an easy lesson for me to learn. I have not learned it once and for all, but instead, have had to test it against the conditions of each moment. Sometimes all I seem to see is my fragile health in further decline. Often it seems that all there is for months and months is unremitting frustration, pain, loss of function, fear, and agony. And then I think, "If that is all I have and all I can expect, the burden seems too much for me to bear."

That is when I have to reassess my relationship with death. If life becomes too much, what then? Do I have a choice? Do I want a choice? If I were to exercise my choice, what effect would it have on those I love? What effect on me and on what my life has come to mean? And what would the mechanics of such a choice be, since I am paralyzed and cannot move?

Is there some other purpose served by suffering that I do not know? Is there somewhere it is registered? Or is the continuing acceptance of meaningless suffering nothing more than foolish masochism? These are the questions before me if I am to face the realities of life and death, as I believe I should.

"Let nature take its course" or "Let God's will be done" has been a formidable guide for people in the past. But today, in matters of life and death, it is impossible to distinguish "God's will" from man's. Medical technology has dramatically changed that.

People who are "dead" from the standpoint of recognizable human activity can nevertheless be kept biologically alive with mechanical "life supports." So living and dying in an urban society is in man's hands now, and has become a matter for public policy, and judicial and medical decisions. No longer is it even a private matter.

That is no mere abstract issue for me, for I have been kept alive by life supports for nearly two thirds of my life. Now the burdens of poor health have reached the point where I must examine these issues in this day's light. Is the choice to live or die up to me, between me and those I love, between me and my God? Am I a thing of public policy, for lawyers to argue about? When I see my medical brethren, do they see me, or do they mainly see their hospital ethics committee and their medical malpractice insurance company?

These are the things that I write about here—the most fundamental of questions: to live or die and, when the choice is made at any given time, how to live and how to die.

FOUR

A Story-Telling Animal

SEEKER: "What is the grand scheme of life?"
WISE MAN: "You're born, you live, and you die."
SEEKER: "You call *that* a scheme?"
WISE MAN: "Actually, most of the scheming comes in during the middle part."

JOHNNY HART, "B.C."

WHAT YOU HAVE READ so far is a story. All collections of words are nothing more than stories, for they are not the real events that occurred. I describe how I feel as accurately as I can, but nevertheless, my words are no more or less than stories that describe how I felt and what I believed at the moments they were written.

Events are neutral, but it is impossible for human beings to perceive events without some degree of interpretation, and that interpretation is determined by the emotions felt at the moment. Moreover, interpretations often change when there is more information, and when seen from various other perspectives.

We are all story-telling animals, even if it is hard for us to accept the idea of it. We prefer to think that we speak only what is true. We hear the stories that others tell and believe them or not. But in serious personal matters, we seem to forget that all stories are subjective truths, and then we are compelled to live our lives as though they were the stories told.

Usually, we tell stories that we ourselves believe. Occasionally we "bend" the truth for a good purpose, not wishing to hurt someone. Sometimes we may do this to gain an advantage. We may feel guilty, and others may consider us to be liars, but we do not usually recognize when we are also deceiving ourselves.

Is there self-deceit in my story about the present state of my health and the implications for my future? Am I taking a group of neutral observations and then telling myself "isn't it awful"?

It all seemed true when I wrote it, but today seems different. I just feel better. The "bowel god" (or goddess) smiled on me today, taking hours off my "start-up" time. My day expanded, I could have a leisurely breakfast and do an hour's work on this book before seeing a patient. I enjoy my time writing, and it always becomes a surprise as I discover new aspects of myself.

I enjoy my work with patients, even when it is difficult. I get a vacation from myself. It absorbs me so completely that I lose all sense of myself in time and space, except as an active participant in my patient's life.

Today was no exception. My patients' concerns became my concerns, and I was no more than a pinpoint of awareness. Of course there are times with patients when something happens that does affect me personally; then I do act out of self-interest. Most of the time, though, I forget myself.

This afternoon Marty and Jim are driving here from Orange County for our monthly lunch. They are my oldest friends; we grew up together there. Marty remained in Orange County and became a successful attorney, heading a firm that includes his wife and four of their five attorney children. Jim lived in New York, where he was a successful newspaper advertising executive, until he retired and returned to Orange County. These monthly lunches last all afternoon.

I really look forward to these get-togethers, and I am proud that Marty and Jim are my friends. It's wonderful to spend time with such good and trusted friends, where there is such a sense of acceptance and openness.

So you can see why today is a "good" day, and why I hardly give any notice to those ominous thoughts about the future of my health. My story today is quite different than it was a few days back, and I am in no hurry to see my life end now. The "ain't it awful" of yesterday is today's "ain't it great."

I have these mood swings, and my mood reflects whatever story I tell myself. Whether it is the story that determines my mood or my mood that determines my story is uncertain in my mind, but it is clear that they go together. It is as though I exist simultaneously in two different worlds, but I can only see the one that has a label on it.

My stories, thoughts, and plans are the windows on the house in which I live, yet I seem to be able to see through only one window at any time. Although I may erroneously think that what I see is all there is, I can actually see only a small part of what is in the house. If I look through another window, I see something entirely different.

I see only a dark abyss through some windows, but through others I can see the wonder and beauty of the universe. Without such story windows, I could not see much meaning in my house at all, so I am very grateful for them.

But I must remember they do not allow me to see the whole house at any one time. To do so, I would have to stand on the Olympian plane, a place reserved only for gods. As a mortal, the best that I have been able to do is keep an open mind—avoiding becoming attached to what I see in only a single window, framed by a single story.

I forget that crucial lesson when I go to a hospital or to see a doctor. I go there with a terrible sense of fear. I anticipate pain, humiliation, and neglect. I expect that the people there will wrest all vestiges of control from me. I feel like a victim.

My fearful behavior often creates a struggle with those I encounter there. While I am certainly not an apologist for everything that goes on in the health care system, I realize that I am the creator of, at the very least, a part of what I experience.

The roots of my fear and the behavior it creates are firmly planted in the three years of hospitalization I had following my acute polio illness. Certainly there were awful things, but somehow those things have erased the other, more positive experiences I also had. And there were many.

Many of my friends were made at that time. Many of the things that make me laugh had their origins in those experiences. I met my wife then, thus making the joys we have had together possible. Indeed, the person I am today can be attributed in large part to those hospital experiences and the growth they produced in me.

But I cannot bear to think I may be hospitalized again. I am much like the veteran whose war experiences were the most important and valued in his life, but who would do almost anything to avoid going through a war again.

When I anticipate an encounter with the health care system, I suddenly forget all that is positive in it, and remember only the terror. Why can I not remember the many kindnesses and the thoughtful care I had there? Why do I always anticipate pain, humiliation, degradation, boredom, and loss of control? Those realities will be there, but why can I see nothing else? Why am I blinded to all other possibilities?

My first experiences with doctors and hospitals were quite different. My first memory of being in a hospital is a very positive one. It was when I was five years old and had my tonsils removed. The principal memory I retain was of the generous provisions of ice cream that were given to post-tonsillectomy patients in those days. The next time I was hospitalized was when I was a medical student, and what I remember primarily about that was the attentive care I received from the student nurses.

Most of my hospital experience, however, has not been as a patient but as a physician, and before that as a medical student. Although the academics of medical school were a grind, I uniformly found great satisfaction in hospital work. I did not mind the long hours, for I always felt they were in a "good cause." I always had the feeling of being useful there, and I thought of hospitals as "good" places. I thought of doctors and nurses as dedicated and good people, too.

Why, then, have those pleasant memories been erased when I encounter a hospital now, and all I see is fear? Perhaps I expected too much, and my expectations were too high and unrealistic. Perhaps, then, when I was disappointed, I was unprepared and devastated.

There is something to the popular accusation that physicians think of themselves as gods. As a physician I felt at the top of the pyramid, and perhaps enjoyed the sense of control too much. Since I saw hospitals and doctors as elevated to some degree, inevitably it reduced the roles of others, and especially those of patients. So it felt like a great fall to go from doctor to patient. It was a loss of too much control, a loss of too much power, a loss of too much pride.

Pride became humiliation, power became impotence and loss of control, elevated status became diminished status, and I became the victim of my own stereotypes. Perhaps my challenge now is to reduce the distance between doctor and patient in my mind, to begin to recognize the humanity in both, that neither one is a god nor a sinner, and neither should be a victim of the other's power.

When I can keep from getting stuck in any one window and realize that I am there for only an instant, I am free and renewed—reborn, as some would say. That seems to happen when I am both absorbed in the action I see in the window and detached from its outcome in a curious way: although I will usually do my best to affect the situation, I know that the outcome is not in my hands.

FIVE

Love or Fear

Love conquers all.

VIRGIL, *Eclogues*

W HEN I WAS twelve years old my family went on vacation to San Francisco. We prepared for weeks before, purchasing new clothes, getting haircuts, and simonizing our car.

By the time we left, it seemed to me that we were the epitome of style and affluence. When we arrived in San Francisco and walked along the street, it seemed that all eyes followed us admiringly as we passed. The warm glow of those childhood memories included the fine hotel in which we stayed, and the excellent restaurant in which we ate. They remained with me as evidences of my privileged childhood.

A decade of experiences later I was living in San Francisco. One day, while I was walking in the Fillmore District, an unseen force drew me into an oddly familiar mid-block hotel. I was puzzled, for there was nothing in its appearance that fit any clear recollection that I had, and it seemed foreign even to any residues of past encounters.

I wandered through the cramped lobby, past a few old regulars. They sat before the front window, staring vacantly through red-rimmed eyes, oblivious to the activity on the sidewalk outside.

The little lobby was filled with faded, styleless, vintage-1930s, overstuffed furniture. A snoozing room clerk hardly noticed as I passed him to climb the narrow staircase to the rooms above. In the upstairs hall, again, I could not grasp what it was that had drawn me to this place. The paint-chipped doors and peeling wallpaper seemed to fit no familiar images in my life.

It was not until light from a half-open doorway pierced the dimly lit hall that memory found its root. Through the doorway I could see the room: iron beds, an enameled dresser, a partly open window. Together they formed a familiar configuration, and memory flooded in. As I stepped inside, the garish picture on the wall confirmed that this was what I feared it was—"the fine hotel" of my family vacation of ten years earlier.

How could it be? How could this rundown place be the fine hotel of my memories? Everything was so different, and yet the same. Could it be that it really had been different, and the years of wear had changed this hotel?

But that was not possible, for the structure of the place, the narrow halls, crowded rooms, and especially the cheap furnishings and art could not be changed by newness and fresh paint. It would still remain a small mid-block hotel, without an elevator, in a seedy part of town. No, it had to be that the meaning of it had been changed by ten years of experience.

I stayed there a long time trying to make sense of the

discrepancies between my memory and what I now saw. I examined small details, looking for clues, only to find that each seemed familiar and strange at the same time.

I searched in vain for the restaurant I remembered with such pride, and found it in the next block. There it was. The name remained unchanged, and I recognized it immediately: The New Yorker. It was a corner coffee shop and delicatessen, open twenty-four hours. It was not and never could have been the restaurant of my memory.

Then I remembered something else that I had forgotten: this was the first and only vacation my family ever took, hardly supportive evidence of the rich and privileged childhood that I remembered, and certainly not making me the envy of all who saw me. Memory became transparent, revealing a very different reality. All seemed to be illusion.

How could my childhood interpretation be so different than it was now? The events had not changed, but my story of what they meant had. Was one story true and the other false? I think not. Instead, they represent different perspectives in time and space. The second viewing of the same events included an additional decade of worldly experiences.

Each story could be said to be true, but only in the context of the moment it was told. The story is frozen in time, while life moves on. Stuck in the past, one is but a set of obsolete responses, a minor Rip Van Winkle.

When the past becomes the future's only map, the opportunities and challenges of today cannot be seen. The rich miser lives like the poor child he once was; a person mistrusts love now, because he missed it in childhood; someone cannot enjoy this moment's peace by reason of the pain once felt.

I think my childhood story about the family vacation reveals a truth larger than any literal recitation of events can suggest, one which transcends time and place. Preoccupation with the accuracy of the details can obscure this larger reality.

I now believe it was that I felt loved in my family. In my child's world, an abundance of love was not different from an abundance of other riches, material or otherwise.

That was the larger and more important truth, one that colored all that I experienced. The quality of the hotel and the restaurant, and the fact that this was our only family vacation, were insignificant when I was bathed in the warmth of feeling loved and of loving my family.

Sometimes that larger truth can be hidden by the story, too. The love that I felt at home was complicated by another emotion, one that often lurks nearby. It causes people to temporize in love. It is jealousy.

One day, when we were both in our forties, my brother and I were talking about our childhood together. I referred to something I assumed was obvious, that my brother had been my father's favorite child.

My brother was shocked, and protested: "No, you were always his favorite. He was always taking you to Catalina."

I could not believe my ears. "He took me there just once," I said, "and it was the only time he ever took me with him anywhere. But I remember that he was always taking you with him to Murrieta Hot Springs."

Amazed, my brother answered, "He took me there once, and it was the only time he ever took me with him anywhere." How could we have had such different perceptions?

At the time these impressions were formed, the universe was very small for us, limited mainly to our family. Even though we participated in the larger world, by far the most important relationships were in the family, and that was where we sought love and the satisfaction of most of our other needs.

We were loved generously, but wanted more, and we were not yet able to get our needs met by others outside the home. My brother and I both must have assumed that if we did not get something we wanted, it was because someone else in our small family universe got it first.

My father loved us both I am sure, but he was not so available because he worked long hours. His lengthy terminal illness further removed him from us. We did not complain, for we knew the facts, but what we felt showed in our discrepant childhood memories. When the universe is small and you have tasted love, you are likely to be afraid that you will lose it, or someone will take it from you.

My old classmate and friend from medical school, Jerry Jampolsky, says there are only two emotions: love and fear. That always seemed too simplistic to me. However, I am beginning to see the wisdom behind it now.

At rock bottom, love and fear do represent two of the most important classes of emotion. A person either contacts the world in an affirming way, out of love, or protects himself fearfully from it. Even anger can be based on fear, and can be an effort to protect oneself from feeling it.

Certainly there is a difference in how I feel when I am fearfully preoccupied with my catalog of physical ailments on the one hand, and when I am absorbed with someone or something in an affirming, loving way on the other—as in the stories that I told.

Ideas like these are helpful, and can keep people from becoming overwhelmed by the complexity of living. Reductionist though it may be, the concept of two basic directions in life has often served a culture well—good and evil, yin and yang. Even Freud divided instincts and drives into two, Eros and Thanatos—those which are life-affirming, and those which move toward death.

The windows of my mind are each a little different, yet similar in certain ways. They make distinct the various feelings I have. There are many frames, but two concern me most: one is labeled "isn't it interesting and great." The other one says, "isn't it empty and awful."

I often have this experience: I will be completely absorbed with what someone is saying about himself, an idea, or something we did together—perhaps even about our relationship. Then, quite to my surprise, he asks, "How could you stand being unable to move?" or "What is it like to be unable to reach for something?"

Why am I surprised when the question—for this person

—seems to follow quite naturally from the discussion? It usually takes me quite a while to respond, but not because I do not want to answer. It's just that it requires me to shift windows, to tell a different story than the one on which I had been focusing.

The window through which I *had* been looking was one that affirmed what was happening at that moment. To answer a question about disability requires looking through a very different window—one that shows what I am *not* doing and *cannot* do. It assumes that instead of being fully involved with my abilities, a part of me is continuously thinking of something else, wishing that I could do more. Thus, what I am able to do is less than my expectations.

Moreover, a negative window is usually further distorted with catastrophic fantasies about the meaning of what is experienced. I know what it is like to be preoccupied with my physical complaints; the pain and discomfort are real. But what bothers me most is what I *think* it means —that it will only get worse, that I will have to go to the hospital, that I will be helpless, and that terrible things will happen to me there. And since I am going to die anyhow, why not do it with as little pain and dislocation as possible? Those are the fantasies with which I embellish the simple reality of pain and discomfort. I become a hypochondriac, and they are my obsessions.

However, I also know what it is like to have pain and discomfort, and yet be so completely engrossed in something I am doing that I am unaware of anything else. Perhaps that is the view of God, to see things as they are, and no more or less. That way everything would be affirmative.

How very different those two positions are—and yet, to a large extent, which one is chosen is arbitrary and potentially volitional. The former is like being stuck in a dreadful hole. In the latter, everything is fine, and I feel like soaring. I would like to treat everything in life and death that way.

SIX

Looking for a Better View

I don't know anybody who can contemplate death and
hum a tune at the same time.

WOODY ALLEN

THERE ARE different windows on the world and different worlds are seen by everyone at different times. One day, you look upon life, family, work, relationships, and see only desolation. Another day you may see a wonderland of joy and beauty, even though the objects remain the same.

When something happens that draws my attention to my body's deterioration and I focus on all that is wrong with me, my world looks very bleak. Recently I had to sign some papers, and I realized I could no longer write my name. In the evening I was unable to sit up for my teeth to be brushed. Then my leg pains seemed much worse, and it seemed as if I was short of breath even when using a respirator. I began to think that the circulatory problems in my legs would require surgery, and of course hospitalization. All of my fears of confinement, helplessness, and pain came to mind, causing me to doubt that I would ever be able to see my patients or ever do anything useful or enjoyable again.

Night is always the worst time. In a dark quiet room

there is nothing to distract me from my inner world. That night I became a hypochondriac. Everything was seen through my gloomy window. How well I know that morbid scenario.

Sometimes I have been down for months and months at a time, yet to my surprise the light has always come eventually. I was confined to lying flat in bed on one such occasion when my back had given out. It was both fragile and fixed, and nothing seemed to help, although in desperation I tried everything—medications, physical therapy, manipulations, acupuncture. Every treatment seemed to make it worse, and bed rest was most dangerous of all. It was hopeless, and each time a doctor looked at my X rays and shook his head, I felt even worse. Lying immobilized in pain made all my other problems worse—breathing, bowels, skin, prostate, circulation in my legs, everything. I was in despair.

My friend Joe came by to cheer me up as he usually could—full of the things he'd done, and funny too. But I was really down that day, and wanted to get away; life seemed too hard. I told him that the struggle was just too much; if it continued this way much longer, I would like to end it all, and I would need help.

Cheerful, generous, wild man Joe said: "You know I would never let you suffer too long." Perhaps this was my chance, I thought, as I sensed that escape might be at hand. I felt overwhelming gratitude for this ultimate offer of friendship and charity. "How would you do it, then?" I asked trustingly.

For a moment he seemed stumped, but ever quick, re-covered his aplomb and unflinchingly responded: "Oh that's easy; I'd just snap your neck." He demonstrated with a quick violent motion and a snapping sound. Joe could never contain his expansiveness, so, feeling he was on a roll and pleased that he had been able to come up with some-thing, he could not stop himself from adding gravely, hop-ing he could get away with it: "After all, I *am* a trained killer."

That was too much—I began to laugh uncontrollably. This was not the tragedy I thought. We were Abbott and Costello, The Two Stooges. I was feeding him straight lines, he was supplying the punch.

Each time I would try to control my laughter, the whole ludicrous tragicomedy would break me up again. And then, as I would see some part of this crazy conversa-tion in a new humorous light, I'd laugh some more. And since my laugh could make no sound without air, it was interspersed with gasps for air, adding to the mixed-up kaleidoscope effect. I laughed and laughed, while tears streamed down my face. Tragedy and comedy tumbled over one another in some form of surreal collage.

All was paradox: friendship expressed by breaking my neck—not quite what I had in mind. Yet, if I wanted to really die, what difference should the method make? Friendly, grandiose, wonderful Joe, who never hurt any-one, carried away by his own words, portraying himself as the trained killer. I suppose that Joe must have seen the

Looking for a Better View • 63

same charade I did, but it hardly matters, for he was laughing just as hard.

No longer did I want to leave this place—it was too much fun. And although I was still bedridden, could still not breathe, and was still uncomfortable, I was now above the fray—watching and enjoying the outrageous farce. Evidently it was not yet my time to go.

Similar events have happened several times before and since. The change often comes from some unexpected place when all seems lost and hopeless. Sometimes there is physical improvement, but usually not. Friends most often bring the change with them, as with Joe. There is something shared that takes effect—humor, tears, a quiet moment—I never know. But something lets me gather strength and elevate my thoughts, as long as I hang in there.

Change may sometimes be so slow that I hardly notice it. One day I realize I am no longer down and have no reason why. I may not have substantially improved physically, but what was "too much to bear" has now become okay—as if that is just the way I am. My back is only slightly better, except I can live with it now.

But I also have learned to take an active part in making the change from looking out the gloomy window to seeing out a far more rewarding one. Knowing how to make the necessary change is very important, because the view from a negative window can become so overwhelmingly oppressive. Here is what I have learned for myself about getting from the darkness to the light.

I have already mentioned that the window frames of

emotion are the stories you tell yourself. What I call my "ain't it awful" stories encase my gloomy window. They sound like this: "Oh, my legs hurt so much, how much can I take? I will have to go to the hospital, and they will operate without success. I cannot stand it; oh, why won't it stop?"

You may notice that just reading those statements has a depressing effect. If you also have had some real pain, you can see what a "downer" it would be. Time drags interminably when I am in that frame of mind, for I am trying to get away from the present where there is life—I am trying to avoid my pain, and yet my attention is almost entirely occupied with my catastrophic expectations, and each makes the other worse.

In order to get into the more positive window, you have to tell yourself stories that will frame what it is you want. Here is what they sound like to me: "Isn't that interesting! Oh, look at the shape, and what unusual colors. I have never seen movement quite like that."

In contrast to the gloomy stories, these deal with what is now observable, and are sensory descriptions of here-and-now reality. I am absorbed with the details of what is happening now, with the anticipation that what is here is something of interest and excitement.

In the negative stories, I do not use my senses—in fact, I try not to, and I am just waiting—I am not looking at anything. I steel myself against what I fear will come. I hate the pain, so I look the other way. My stories do not support becoming absorbed in life, but are guides to avoiding it. No wonder life seems unbearable and hopeless!

My attitude when looking through the positive window is that of a natural observer—I could be observing birds, artwork, traffic patterns, or perhaps even some aspect of myself. But I must have the proper window frame to support the desired view.

To see through the affirmative window, the story I tell myself must be interesting and valuable. It must help to open my eyes to see more—more details of form, shape, color, and movement. "Look at that! Did you hear that? It's remarkable."

Is it really possible to change the story and the window? You may protest that you could never do that with pain, or you may say that to tell a story that does not reflect how you feel would be "phony" and inauthentic.

And, of course, in acute and overwhelming distress, all volition may well be stripped away. However, in most situations the same contents can be viewed in very different ways, with very different effects. The main question, then, is whether you prefer the greater interest of looking through window A to the gloom of window B.

You cannot tell yourself, "It's dull, I can't stand it, and I can't wait for it to be over," and expect to find something interesting and absorbing. "Seek and ye shall find," says the ancient wisdom. So you must be clear about what you are looking for.

Thus the first task in getting to the positive view is to tell the right story. That requires listening to the words and stories you silently tell yourself, as well as what you say out loud. Then you must be willing to tell another story that is consistent with what you want.

Another quality associated with the positive window is "losing yourself in it." You have to let the object of your observations absorb you. Paying very close attention to details usually helps, especially any changes you notice. People are, of course, the most naturally interesting subjects, so being with them is also helpful. Listening attentively to people and watching them carefully is almost synonymous with that kind of absorption.

You need to actively participate too, because activity is characteristic of the positive window, while passivity goes with the negative one. Asking questions and disclosing your own reactions promotes involvement. Again, do everything you can to become involved with your subject.

When the world seems depressing, my interest is almost entirely in myself. When trying to get out of the desolation, I have to lose my preoccupation with myself, and even my awareness of myself, in favor of the objects of my observation. When I can look with eagerness on what I see, I recognize the wonder and joy in the world.

Of course, it is hard to see clearly if the subject under study is my personal pain. That I say "my pain" already begins to cloud the window, since observer and observed are no longer on opposite sides of the pane/pain, but the same one.

So it may seem contradictory to suggest that I can lose myself with positive interest in my own pain, but it is not.

When looking through the dark window, my principal concern is with how the pain affects me as a person, and how it will affect me in the future. In the window of light it is the characteristics of the object alone that attract me; it is as though the window has been washed clean, and the view is sharp and clear. I do not feel personally involved any longer, even though the pain comes from inside my own body.

To see through an affirmative window, changing the words and stories you tell yourself may be enough. If not, becoming involved in the details of sensory observation may do it. But if you still feel stuck, there are other things you can do to shake loose.

Because you want to lose yourself and become engrossed in the subject of your observation, you may find it useful to assume the identity of what you are watching. If you are with another person, try to imagine what it is like to be that person, what he might be saying silently to himself. Try to get inside his skin, and out of yours.

You can even do the same thing with a bird or an inanimate object like a car. It requires a little more imagination, because birds and cars don't usually talk; however, it is worth the effort, as a means of getting out of yourself. You may think it's foolish, but it is no more foolish than staying stuck in a gloomy world.

Sometimes I imagine that I am my pain, and I think of what it would be like to be the one that produces that pain, rather than being the victim of it. I get a rest from being a victim that way, and sometimes I discover surprising things.

Almost anything you can do actively will help to get you out of being stuck in the "down" position. The most important thing is to keep trying and experimenting. Sooner or later you will hit upon a method for liberating yourself.

The value of abandoning preoccupation with oneself may seem questionable to some people though, because there is so much contemporary emphasis on a strong sense of self. It is considered a virtue, and we tend to think it's only natural to be primarily concerned with "number one." It is more of a paradox than a contradiction, though, because a strong sense of self is usually associated with a strong commitment to something outside of oneself.

A person who is confident of who he is can become fully involved with others or the affairs of the world without feeling in danger of losing his identity. By contrast, the person with a fragile sense of self fears that it may be lost or taken away when not protected. Hence, he is constantly vigilant.

For the masses of people, a sense of self is a fairly recent historical development. Before the seventeenth century most people thought of themselves in the same way that they were regarded by others—as subordinate to a group, clan, caste, or class. The concept of individual rights had not yet become a part of everyday consciousness, and most people did not consider events primarily in an individual context.

While the development of self-interest has brought great advantages over the old ways, preoccupation with oneself has also become a major source of unhappiness. People seem always to want and expect more than they have, so they are chronically unhappy.

By contrast, most religions, perhaps all, teach that the road to salvation, peace, and happiness is through selflessness: "Give much, expect little," "Dedicate your life to God," "Serve mankind," and many others. The message is that you should become absorbed in life through active participation with others.

One final problem is that when you are in the dark window, you tend to forget that the other one ever existed, and so getting out never enters your mind. Sometimes you just do not seem to have the energy for anything more than vegetation. But once you have the experience of being able to change windows, you are more likely to recognize it as an ever-present possibility.

In spite of the obvious advantages of looking through the window in which you will see beauty and happiness, sometimes you just do not want to, and would prefer the desolation window. It is as though you want to see how far down you can go, how much you can "get away with." It is strange, but true. Why would anyone prefer to wallow in the darkness of pain, regret, fear, and emptiness? Yet, so many of us do.

SEVEN

Soon the Leaves Will Fall

Death is nature's way of telling you
it is time to slow down.

THE FIRST TIME I heard a clergyman at a funeral say something like "Rejoice, for she goes to a better place and to her reward," I was puzzled. I looked around to see if anybody there was rejoicing, and as I suspected, they were not.

Most of the people who were assembled believed in an afterlife, I am quite sure. They believed that the deceased —good person that she was—was on her way to heaven. Yet there was no joy, not even a flicker of a smile.

I was still young, and still believed in authority and that "there must be a reason for everything." So I finally concluded that they were so preoccupied with their grief and the loss they felt, that they just were not ready to feel the joy. I had my doubts, nevertheless, because most were not so self-centered that they would not feel some pleasure associated with losses for them that would have beneficial effects for others, as for example, when their children left them for "a better place" like school, work, or marriage. Somehow this was very different.

But there was an even more contradictory part of it:

you were "supposed to be sad." What would people think of you if you actually did smile and rejoice at a funeral? Probably that you were callous or crazy. It would be considered wholly inappropriate.

My father's funeral was filled with those contradictions —relief that his suffering was over, joy that the rest of the family was together again, and later an episode of senseless rage. All of it beyond my comprehension.

And when I was young, I often had an overwhelming feeling that I was about to laugh at sad things like death. Once in the seventh grade a teacher was talking with much feeling about a death in her family. Jimmy, the boy who sat next to me, began to laugh—doing everything he could to stifle it. Then Richard, who sat in front of him, began, and I could no longer stop myself.

Our teacher was deeply hurt, having shared something of profound significance to her. She considered us terribly disrespectful. I felt awful and ashamed; as I found out later, so did Jimmy and Richard. After that I was afraid that I might inappropriately laugh if things became very serious. I know now that such feelings are quite common as a means of denial, but I did not know it then.

The loss of someone is awful, and filled with awe. The pain is palpable, and comes in overwhelming waves. Grief is as inexplicably painful as anything I have felt—it is relentless, and it seems that it will never end. It is sad. It is heartbreaking. It is wretched.

Yet that is not all it is, either. Sometimes the pain is prolonged by thinking any other emotions are inappropriate and wrong. There are others there, just the same, and they, too, come in waves. Why not some laughter now and then, why not some gentle lightness with the gloom? That is how people are.

There is a danger in insisting that death is only grim. People can become accustomed to avoiding joy until it becomes a habit. They can get stuck in one dark unpleasant place, and never learn to see the light of day again. Death is without reason, so all or any of the feelings can be there.

When my brother died, I felt like wood. I did what I had to do, yet I did not feel the depth of sadness that I knew must be there. The service was nearly over, and I had been respectful while not feeling very much. Then someone spoke to me of him, something quite ordinary, and there was a trigger there: I began to sob and sob—as though I might never stop. And when I finally did, what I felt was new, simple, clear appreciation, without regret.

What I feel, if not foreclosed by what I expect, can be very surprising and at times revitalizing. That is even true when death and dying are the issues. I have thought the end was near many times. Then, to my surprise, something would change again, and I would have a fresh perspective. One can never know until the time arrives. A case in point is in the experience of one of the young men who helped me at one time.

He was sailing in the Great Lakes, when a powerful freak storm hit the area. He was swept from the boat into the turbulent waters. The waves washed over him, making swimming impossible, and there seemed little hope of rescue from his friend still in the boat.

He went under several times and all seemed lost. In despair, he felt sure that he would die. He expected, as he had heard would happen, to have the most significant events of his life "flash before his eyes." Instead, what he saw were the most banal of television commercials, one by one slowly played before him.

Distracted from his plight momentarily by the irony and surprise of what he saw, he felt buoyed, and his strength renewed. Despair turned to hope, and so he struggled on much longer than he thought he could. Then the storm abated for a moment, long enough for him to see his boat and friend approach. And he was saved.

If you prejudge what life and death are and can be, you limit their possibilities and your potential. Death and being near to death are crucial times, and are not necessarily so grim. The cult movie *Harold and Maude* is a story of these possibilities.

Harold, a youth surrounded by privilege and wealth, enjoys none of it, and instead is preoccupied with death. Disturbed and depressed, he surrounds himself with death symbols, and often tries out methods of suicide. He turns the elegant sports car he is given into a hearse, and his main activity is attending the funerals of people he does not know.

At one anonymous funeral he meets Maude, who is nearly eighty. Like Harold, she enjoys going to funerals. But she is a free spirit, despite having survived death-camp horrors, and she eccentrically celebrates each day—death reminding her of life's transitory nature. Opposites in age, in background, in outlook, and in mood, it is on the grounds of death they meet.

Maude provides meaning to Harold's empty life, and he falls in love with her. He seems happy for the first time. But Maude says that eighty years is long enough to live, and it is time for her to leave. She and Harold enjoy a party to celebrate her eightieth birthday. At the end, she takes poison and bids him a fond goodbye. In panic at her loss, Harold rushes her to the hospital, trying to save her. But it is futile.

Harold's anguished grief turns to desperation. He takes his sports-car-turned-hearse and drives furiously. He drives and drives, out into the country, as fast as he can, out onto an open area to a high cliff above the ocean. Not slowing one bit, the car hurtles over the cliff and crashes on the rocky shore below. Harold has seemingly joined his beloved.

But as we see the cliff again, to our surprise there is Harold, evidently having escaped at the last moment. He turns his back and walks away, joyfully kicking his heels together as he goes.

Life and death, together and apart, celebration and despair, life leading to death and death to life and rebirth—these are the ever-renewing cycles of time.

And time is all we have, not as a possession, for it cannot be captured, but as a means of our awareness. For the young it goes so slowly; they have too much, so they waste and squander it. For the old it goes too fast, so they try to hold it back and stem its tide.

Yet, whatever we do with it, it moves relentlessly on. So the best we can really do is to join with its inexorable flow. And when we do, we synchronize with something more than us, something larger than we can know. We join the endless tides of eternity.

The seasons come and go. The green leaves of the spring turn lush in summer. In the autumn they turn to orange and brown, and then must fall to lie dormant in the wintertime. When the spring returns, new leaves draw their nourishment from those that came before.

Does it matter that one leaf falls before another from the tree? Secure that each season will again reappear, ripen, then fade and fall away, we *are* the rhythms of the earth and sea. Eventually all the leaves will fall, must fall, to nourish the next renewal, each in its own special way. And when they do, there is no end.

EIGHT

People and Technology

And now I see with eye serene
The very pulse of the machine.

WORDSWORTH,
"She Was a Phantom of Delight"

I OWE A LOT to technology. My life, for example, since machines keep me alive. But it has been a love-hate relationship. I hate the way technology has made life impersonal in so many ways.

When I need to talk to someone about something, it makes me crazy to get an answering machine instead. It reduces me to a category and I have no opportunity to explain any of the details of life that make me human.

"If your call is regarding a new subscription, press one; if it is about your bill, press two; if it is about a renewal, press three."

"My call has nothing to do with a subscription or a bill, but this is the only number listed in the telephone directory for your company. Can I talk to a person, please?"

Silence, followed by a dial tone!

I can find some humor and irony in how technology frustrated me in that telephone conversation—but only if I can find some live person to share it with.

I find no humor, however, when I contemplate how technology can create some grim situations. I hate the way that technology has come between doctor-patient relationships and how it has become a substitute for the human contact in nurse-patient relationships. And I hate how it sometimes keeps people hopelessly alive in agony when they could die in peace. I get depressed when I see the human wastelands that store the elderly, disabled, and ill—in convalescent hospitals, board-and-care homes, and such.

Although proponents of technology have always said it will free people from mundane tasks so they can have more time for personal interaction, the opposite usually seems to happen. People seem to spend more time in isolation from one another, attending to machines instead—driving alone in their cars, watching television while ignoring the presence of others, talking impersonally on the telephone, and lots of other similar ways.

Thus it was with the utmost ambivalence that I entered the computer age. I had serious doubts that a computer could do anything but further complicate my life and I resisted the idea for years in spite of encouragement by friends.

I began to seriously consider it because of the twelve to fourteen hours a day I spend in the iron lung, alone and bored. I cannot do anything requiring movement because of my paralysis and because I am encased in the steel tank. To read would require that someone constantly stand by to turn pages for me and talking on the telephone is difficult because my breath works against the movement of the iron lung, creating a curious halting quality in my voice.

What I *can* do is listen to recordings of books and watch

television (I am no longer bothered that everything is seen backwards through a mirror). Unfortunately, all television begins to look alike to me after a while and I just feel numb.

So, I longed to be involved more actively and although having people with me constantly was the best solution, it was not altogether practical. A second-best alternative might be to get a computer that would enable me to do some work during my "dead time" in the iron lung.

The way that I was used to writing, whether notes, letters, articles, or books, was by dictating onto a cassette and then having a typist transcribe it. I would redictate from what was typed for the next draft, or as many times as necessary to get it right—for letters just once or twice, but for articles and books six to twelve or more times. A more skilled writer could no doubt be more efficient, but I am only as skilled as I am, and that is what I have to live with.

I thought that with a computer I might be able to do some editing while lying in the iron lung. Perhaps I could view a monitor overhead and electronically correct drafts I had dictated, instead of dictating so many different times.

I looked into voice-activated systems but found large problems. The iron lung distorted my voice in different ways each time I was in it, making the results unreliable and, anyhow, voice technology has a long way to go before it is perfected.

Then I found some software that would show a replica of a keyboard on the monitor. By puffing or sipping on a straw placed in my mouth or by using a one-finger switch, I could start and stop a little light that would designate a letter or number. Then using the same straw or switch, I could strike the letter or number. It was tediously slow and very expensive but possible.

Now, this probably sounds as if I knew what I was doing, but nothing could be farther from the truth. First of all, just the idea of a computer in my life produced waves of panic in me. Then, trying to understand the bizarre foreign language of data processing seemed an insurmountable task. Finally, I had no interest in the technology, beyond the possibility of it making my life easier and more efficient. These were not ideal attitudes for beginning.

Since everybody told me the Macintosh computer is the easiest kind to operate—"user friendly," they said—I rented one for a week to try out the software system. It was, indeed, user friendly and I was calling it "Mac" almost immediately. But friendliness is not everything in the computer game, as it turns out. I also found the screen was too small for me to see well, and to buy a larger screen would cost as much as the computer itself.

Besides, the friend who did my typing used other equipment, not compatible with the Macintosh, so I would not be able to read on my computer what she had typed on hers. I could be compatible either with her or with the friendly Macintosh, but not with both. Despite the reassurances of salesmen, I learned that in the friendly world of computers, nothing is compatible with much of anything.

The only compatibility I felt was with the friends who

had been advising me, and they were unbelievably patient and generous with their time and information. So, as an act of desperation, and as a means of further fostering compatibility with my computer friends, I took the plunge. I bought an IBM clone (for the uninitiated like me, that means a cheaper computer that uses IBM technology and can use IBM software) that was inexpensive enough that I could stand to have the whole project fail.

My friends installed the software necessary to begin and left me with the operating manuals to get started. Frankly, I was unwilling to spend any of my precious time out of the iron lung reading such dull literature. So the manuals and the computer remained side by side and idle for a week, until my friends made up a few notes that would allow me to start on my own.

Before getting a monitor installed on my iron lung, a cumbersome task at best, I thought I had better get to know the beast a bit while I was in my wheelchair. That way I could see it from different sides and angles, something that I have always found helpful.

You see, since I have been immobilized, I am disoriented in space. My spatial orientation seems tied to actively manipulating things and moving around them. For example, I am mystified by how to fix something unless it can be placed in my hand and turned around. I have an appalling sense of direction unless I can drive my electric wheelchair where I am going. I need active involvement with something to grasp how it works.

I sat in front of the lighted monitor and serendipity! I

discovered, to my amazement, that I could use the keyboard with my one pretty good finger. There I was in front of the monitor, punching keys like a regular human being! The keys required a much lighter touch than on a typewriter and if I were positioned just right, I could let gravity drop my finger on a key.

But the joy was short-lived, since I can breathe for only a few minutes while sitting up. I tried my usual lying-down position, but it did not work: gravity was against me in using my finger and I could not see the keyboard.

The only alternative if I had to sit up was a respirator—another bit of technology required by my new computer use. So, I used a portable respirator that pumps air in and out of a tube which I hold in my mouth or a rubber bladder that is bound against my abdomen. Both methods simulate normal breathing.

One problem was solved, but another was created. It took a couple of weeks before I could get used to sitting up and using the respirators all day. I had a lot of resistance to the idea of being attached to machines nearly all day and night. Having some hours free of machines gave me some illusory sense that I was stronger than I really am, and it's hard to give up supportive illusions even if you are pretty sure they *are* only illusions.

It was very difficult also to learn how the beast itself worked. I treated it as though one false move and it would attack and devour me. Every time I typed in something, it seemed as if I would make a mistake and erase it.

I amazed my friends with my capacity to get into

gridlock, a condition in which everything is stuck and the only way out is to turn the whole thing off and begin again. Of course, I would lose all of my work in the process. That was the first evidence I showed of creativity at the computer. I discovered innovative ways of getting into gridlock that were previously unknown to man.

Each time this or some other disaster would occur, I would call my friends and, bless them, they were never exasperated by my stupidity, although they had every reason to be. I often called them two or three times a day. In spite of this generous help, I began to feel that the whole adventure was a failure and, as I had feared, it had only complicated my life further instead of helping it. It looked as if it might be nothing but a waste of time and money.

I would have given up after the first month, but for the persistent encouragement of my friends. It was, of course, a painfully slow process. But soon I could feel myself becoming slowly more efficient, to my surprise.

Before I knew what was happening, I was no longer waiting for typed drafts to be returned for redictation, but actually typing and editing them at the same time. The fifteen minutes I started spending with the computer was extended to an hour, then two, and even three or four sometimes.

Although I typed very slowly with my one awkward finger, in a couple of months the whole process of writing was quicker and more efficient. I really made only one draft now, which I could revise as necessary. I felt closer to the material and I could always see where I was. (When I used to dictate, I would tend to lose my place and ramble). Before I realized what was happening, I had stopped dictating entirely and was doing my own typing. I could not have dreamed it would be so!

The effect of this new activity on my entire life was nothing short of miraculous. It happened so subtly that I could only recognize it in retrospect. I must have been depressed for months before, because after a couple of months of "computer therapy," it was as though someone pulled up the shades. I realized that I had been seeing the world through a gray fog and now the sun was shining.

It is difficult for me to describe what it was like: for almost forty years, the whole time I had been disabled, I had to wait for others before I could do anything at all. Now, as soon as I was in my electric wheelchair, wearing a respirator, I was free and on my own. I did not have to wait for anyone.

I could now drive up to my computer keyboard, press a single button that turned on the whole system, call up whatever file I wanted, and work entirely on my own. I could write an article, send a letter, work on this book, check my finances. I could now reach out to the world instead of waiting for it to reach me.

I no longer had to wait, and wait, and wait, and wait, and wait, and wait, and wait for everything. I felt a new level of control in my life—it felt like *my* life.

And I no longer felt depressed, although I had not realized I had been.

Understand this: I had accepted my lot, my need to

wait, and most people were very good about helping. What I had not realized was that each time I waited, I died a minor death of the spirit, until I was eroded into the insulated state we call depression.

Now I could not wait to get up in the morning, so I could get to the keyboard! People were as likely to wait for me now as I was for them, because I could work on my own. I was completely absorbed—in love, the engagement that cures all.

It was *not* by any means the computer that I loved, not at all. It was the business of my life that absorbed me. The difference was that I could get at it now. It was that the computer provided me with more direct access to my life's business. I had only enough interest in the technology itself to allow me to get at my work.

Remarkably, it did other things for me as well, things that completely surprised me. Not only did my mental health improve, but so did my physical health. Sitting erect more than before was like a form of exercise, and I was able to endure its discomfort because I was so lost in what I was doing.

It was also a great boon to my shameful old nemesis, my bowels. Sitting up more seemed to help my regularity. So to the constipated of the world, I offer this bold new program, throw away your laxatives and buy a computer. (Offer not guaranteed!)

But the road to romance inevitably has its potholes. After only a few months of blissful union with my computer, I had to face the heartbreak of separation. My companion was taken ill, and it looked serious! Its floppy disk drive was in a state of complete collapse and I fell into despair. Home remedies were useless and you know how doctors are these days. Finally I found an old-fashioned one who made house calls.

That is when I really got worried. He said that major surgery was required and it meant hospitalization. With a tear in my eye we bid farewell. The image of its departure remains in my mind as though it were yesterday—my friend lying helplessly on the back seat of the computer doctor's car. Partly dismantled, it did not even look like the one I had come to love. I tried to console myself with "it's better to have loved and lost . . ."

During its absence I wandered aimlessly through the house; a wave of remorse swept over me whenever I passed its favorite haunts, now empty. The doctor called to say that an organ transplant was required; he acknowledged the seriousness of the procedure, but expressed reserved optimism.

But miraculously, the plucky little fellow accepted the new disk drive as his own without complications and was returned home ahead of schedule. We were united once again.

I had worried because it was not covered in my health insurance policy, but it turned out to still be under warranty. The whole procedure, including hospitalization, was free. Too bad I never had one of those warranties for myself, things might have been a lot easier.

My computer gave me new life by providing me with the means of getting *at mine.*

I can understand how people develop relationships with machines that are as intense as those with people. It's getting harder and harder to get close to people and my computer is the best way I know of getting close to myself.

With tongue in cheek, I wrote in a letter to a friend of mine, "Now that I found God in the computer monitor, I am going to buy one for my wife. That way through modem we can have deep spiritual communication."

Even though it was my joke, I feel offended by it. I take my spiritual matters too seriously to trivialize them. But that is the point—that what is available and right in front of my nose, I sometimes complicate and travel great distances to find. My computer allowed me a hitherto unavailable directness in important communication, but I dare not allow it to replace what I can already have, even better, without it.

As you can see, I have not lost my ambivalence about technology. If it is available, it will be used, even when it may become an obstacle to the very thing you were trying to achieve in the first place. Medical technology was created for lofty humane purposes, but it now creates suffering as much as relieves it.

I hope that with my new-found computer pleasures, I can keep myself from going into "overkill" and not allow it to keep me from more important matters.

The most important lesson is that life is full of surprises and you never know when, why, or how good things will happen. Even when you have given up hope that things can get better, they may appear in entirely unexpected ways. You have to be open to the unexpected, otherwise you can miss the best parts of life.

Oh, by the way, the road to romance not only has potholes, but "pottyholes" as well. My computer bowel solution did not last long. I went through a desperate period when nothing worked at all. The doctors I consulted did their best, but to no avail, and I got quite sick.

But then I had to eat my technology-ambivalent words! A nondoctor who was having a similar problem invented a machine that bypassed my difficulty. Just plug me in and in less than an hour I was successfully finished with what used to take me half a day, usually without success.

Just so I do not mislead anyone, the machine is far from being as efficient and satisfactory as the device God designed—even when His creation is not working well—but in my desperate straits (no pun intended), it has been a great boon.

NINE

A Time for Everything: A Time to Die

For everything there is a season, and a time
  for every matter under heaven:
a time to be born, and a time to die;
a time to plant, and a time to pluck up what
  is planted;
a time to kill, and a time to heal;
a time to break down, and a time to build up;
a time to weep, and a time to laugh;
a time to mourn, and a time to dance;

a time to cast away stones, and a time to
    gather stones together;
a time to embrace, and a time to refrain from
    embracing
a time to seek, and a time to lose;
a time to keep, and a time to cast away;
a time to rend, and a time to sew;
a time to keep silence, and a time to speak;
a time to love, and a time to hate;
a time for war, and a time for peace.
What gain has the worker from his toil?

Ecclesiastes 3:1–9

IS THERE a right time for each of these events to occur, as Ecclesiastes tells us? Is there a right time for each of us to die? If there is, how are we to know?

Many people think there is no time right for dying, and that there never will be one. For them death is a failure in the life cycle, not a part of it. For them, life is a game, a competitive sport, in which to die is to lose, and they want only to win.

In our sports-oriented society we admire only those who win, and who refuse to *ever* give up. We think the same game is still being played when it has been over for a long time, and a new one with different rules has begun. We seem to have forgotten that there is a time for giving up gracefully, and being "good sports."

We may be remembered in history as the society whose most enduring philosophy emerged from a coach's simplistic and self-serving statement, designed to exploit his players: the absurd "winning isn't everything, it's the only thing." We have become a society that admires its sports figures more than its political, religious, and scientific leaders, preoccupied with celebrity status instead of good deeds.

So indoctrinated, everyone becomes a "loser"—if not now, soon. People equate death with losing, and so cling to life, whatever its quality, as a miser hoards gold. They become "time misers," holding on to biological life when it has ceased to have usefulness, even though biology is only the meagerest evidence of being alive, and requires no purpose or meaning.

Does an extra week, an extra month, or even an extra year of meaningless existence really put you ahead in what we spuriously call the "game of life," or is that just an illusion created to justify a continuation of the uselessness?

Life is no game! And it cannot be judged by even the most sophisticated won-and-lost column in a box score. Life is certainly a great deal more than that. To reduce life to something that can be counted assures that its richness will be missed.

Doing so would make us oblivious to the wonder of a starry night, a blazing moment of new comprehension, the excitement of loving, and the fullness of being loved— there would be no place for these and so many more of the awesome experiences of living that dwarf the narrow idea of winning and losing into irrelevance. So, for that matter, would we miss the horror of cruelty or senseless tragedy, and the empty awfulness of death.

Yet, in our culture death continues to be treated as a defeat, a blight on the box score of life. We are taught "never give up"—as in the popular movie and television stories where the apparently dead or defeated hero arises phoenixlike to "snatch victory from the jaws of defeat." Our heroes are Rocky, Rambo, and Chuck Norris when they are not Magic Johnson, Wayne Gretzky, or John Elway, whose glory days are brief at best.

These attitudes are so deeply ingrained in our society, that we are surprised when we learn that they have ever been different. But in fact, most non-technological cultures recognize death to be of equal importance with other life phases.

Cultures that remain in touch with nature's rhythms welcome death "when the time has come." On the day they called "a good day to die," American Indians had rituals to summon and greet the end. They were ready to bow gracefully to death as an inevitable developmental stage.

Even for the Victorians, dying well was considered the necessary culmination of a good life. They prepared meticulously for final deathbed scenes, with carefully drawn, pithy statements to be uttered in the presence of just the right family members and friends. They made death a vital part of life.

To deny that death is a part of the life cycle, as birth, growth, maturity, and reproduction are, is to live unrealistically. And what are the consequences if we do refuse to accept the reality of death?

People who hate jogging are out doing it each day. Millions are spent each year on face-lifts, "tummy tucks," and wrinkle removal, just to create the illusion that people are not growing old. Millions of vitamin capsules are consumed each day in the hope of living longer. People have themselves cryogenically frozen when they die, hoping for a medical miracle that will one day bring them back to life.

How much time and energy is taken from other worthy purposes in the vain pursuit of an immortality of the flesh? A man whose body survives a hundred years may have lived much less than one who dies for a noble cause when young. The only true means of approaching immortality is by contributing to the future of mankind.

Those who try to remain young when they are not are consumed with the kind of love Narcissus had, a love limited and brief in time, affecting them and them alone. By contrast, the effects of Mother Teresa's love of others will endure long beyond her lifetime, and is thus eternal.

The seasons come and go with regularity; we play our parts willingly or grudgingly. Each season has its tasks—birth and growth with spring, full flowering in the summer, maturity in autumn, and consolidation and death in winter. The seasons come and go and we will do our parts. Still, sometimes we seem not to know what the season is.

On April 22, 1977, an event occurred, one so powerful that I remember it as clearly as if it just happened. It shook every rational belief that I held, and told me a change of season was near.

I was awakened at 6:30 A.M. by a stentorian voice that intoned: "You have fifteen hundred more days!" But to my astonishment, no one was standing beside me. My wife, the only other person in the room, was still sleeping.

I had never heard a voice come out of the blue like this before, and what a frighteningly awesome voice it was. My immediate thought was that it must be the voice of God, a remarkable thought for one who does not believe in any conventional religious ideas.

My next thought was of the meaning of the message. "It must be," I thought, "that I will die in fifteen hundred days." Needless to say, it was a very sobering thought.

My daily routine began as usual, as soon as the man who helps me with it arrived. Although I went through the motions of going to the bathroom, being dressed, and being lifted into my wheelchair, I remained completely preoccupied with what the voice had said. While my routine was in progress, I mentally calculated just when my last day would be, and began to think what all of this might mean.

When I was able to confirm the date of my last day, my astonishment grew even more. Taking into account the leap year that would intervene, I was shocked to realize that my predicted death date was also the anniversary of my brother's death four years earlier. That day seemed very significant to me, since my brother had been my guide through life, and I had missed him terribly.

Whoever had spoken to me seemed to have done some careful arithmetic to come up with that date. But I did not believe in an anthropomorphic god, much less one that does arithmetic. Nevertheless, those were the facts, and they could not be denied no matter how bizarre they seemed—and they certainly did seem bizarre to me.

I did my best to be rationally scientific about it, and to remember that I am a psychiatrist. I am quite familiar with hallucinations. Patients almost always believe the voices they hear are "real," so I was not unusual in that respect— just, perhaps, psychotic.

I also know that what is unconscious has its own rules and power, and that could account for a great deal. Creative solutions to complex problems often come directly from the unconscious, but to my knowledge it does not know how to do linear arithmetic calculations.

I was shaken by the experience, for something had happened to me that did not fit my rational frame of mind. Not knowing what else to do, I carefully recorded what had happened, and began the long wait until the appointed day, to discover if it had been a true prophecy.

I told only a few close friends about it, and got a variety of responses. Some were reassuring: "Maybe it does not mean you will die, but that something else will happen, maybe something good," or "Well, now you can plan how you will spend the remainder of your life; it is a gift."

But most people offered rational explanations: "It was just a hypnagogic hallucination," or "It must have been something you ate." A few were sympathetic, and a few looked at me as if I were quite mad. Their comments reflected the spectrum of my own thoughts.

As is often typical of me, I considered all of the possible explanations, but had a hard time choosing any one over the others. So, also typically, I decided to be practical about it. "Okay," I thought, "if this may be a prophecy, how does that affect how I live?"

That answer was clear. I had better start living the way I wanted and *at each moment,* without putting things off. That meant that I had to do and be what I thought worthwhile, starting right now. It was not an entirely new thought, but now I felt some real urgency about it.

Many people may wonder, "What is the big deal about that?" Well, it was a big deal for me, because ever since I became disabled, I had been playing "catch-up," trying to prove to myself and the world that I was as good as other people, and could do most anything they could do.

I was competing with everyone who was able bodied. Very often I would try to act as if I did not need help when I did, so I was in considerable pain and discomfort. The only person I had been fooling, though, was myself, because I could not hide my disability; it was obvious.

I also did too many things out of fear and insecurity. Since I got sick I have been afraid of getting in "over my head," so I have been unnecessarily cautious in a lot of ways. I stayed in jobs longer than necessary, doing things I no longer wanted to do or believed in.

I was not afraid of being dead, but I was afraid of the process of getting there. Helplessness, vulnerability, weakness, and being at the mercy of others were my fears. They were epitomized by a recurrent fantasy that I had: I am alone in a skid row hotel room; a single bare bulb dimly lights the room; under the bulb is the only piece of furniture—the iron bed in which I lie, unable to move. I am helpless, hungry, uncomfortable, and lonely. From time to time dangerous looking characters open my door to look in menacingly at me. I am afraid of what they might do to me.

In order to avoid the realization of that fantasy, I had lived cautiously and protectively, as if catastrophe might strike at any time. I could never have enough money, friends, or family to provide the kind of safety net I wanted.

Eventually catastrophe probably would strike, but my voice of prophecy reminded me that it could happen any-time. So if I could die tomorrow or in fifteen hundred days, I did not want to live all of my life in *preparation* to live. It was time to live now.

Having been shocked into that realization by the disem-bodied voice that spoke to me, I did begin to live differ-ently—with more discrimination, commitment, and en-thusiasm. It was great, but as is also typical of me, in a few weeks I forgot about it and returned to my old form.

However, this was not an ordinary voice. Whoever it belonged to knew me all too well and concluded that I needed a reminder. So about two months later it gave me one. Once again, early one morning, I was startled awake by the voice. This time it was brief and straight to the point: "You have very little time left!"

I could no longer fool around, for it seemed someone was both watching and watching over me. I began living again with a heightened awareness of the preciousness of life. This time it also resulted in a major concrete action that was long overdue.

I was the director of an educational and research center for social and community psychiatry which I had started several years before. It was a great place to work, giving me interesting colleagues, important work, security, and a good salary. As the boss, I had some power and prestige, and I could do my own teaching and research.

There was just one problem: in spite of all of the advantages, my heart was no longer in it. For one thing, the administrative activities had begun to bore me, and I disliked the required details of maintenance. When I had started the center, I was deeply committed to its mission and fully absorbed in making it work. The job had changed some, but even more important, I had changed, and I was at a different stage in my life.

When I was really honest with myself, I could see that I was just hanging on for all the wrong reasons: I thought it made me look good, it gave me some petty power over others, and it gave me a feeling of security.

I was in the middle of a lot of action, and I was in demand for speaking, teaching, and various community activities. For example, I was a member of several boards of directors in related organizations, and I spent a lot of time making deals. Once that had been exciting for me and shielded me from feeling alone, but now it was mainly just an onerous task.

When I was brutally frank with myself, I could see another important reason for making a change. It was something that should have been obvious, but that I did not want to admit. My health had declined, and I was no longer up to the physical demands of doing the job well, so I had been "cutting corners." Travel had become very difficult, and I no longer had enough energy for evening meetings.

The political enthusiasm for community mental health was in decline, and programs were in disarray. More than ever the center needed a strong leader. Although I could have continued indefinitely, I was not the right person to provide the necessary leadership any longer. As soon as I was able to extricate myself, with many regrets, I left.

With the energy I had remaining, I began doing only things I wanted to do, things that I felt competent to do, and things that I placed value on. Seeing patients, teaching, and writing were among them. When I was doing them, I felt "all there," not only half there as I had felt sometimes in my job before. Only in retrospect could I see how much of my time had been spent in ways that kept me from feeling lonely, or that made me feel I looked good.

Stopping all that was like feeling a fresh breeze on my face, for I was no longer hiding behind organizational position and power. I was now standing on my own.

Leaving my job at the center meant that I made less money, had less security and prestige, missed having a staff to help me, and was more often lonely. But I felt better, because I was being true to myself.

Also, I was fully absorbed in what I did, so absorbed

that I stopped watching the calendar. I did not realize it when my fifteen hundred days had passed. By the time I did check my notes against the calendar again, it was several months past the date I had assumed I would die.

Someone once said that life is what happens to you while you are making other plans. That certainly seemed true for me. And here I was materially poorer, in declining health, without the advantages of organizational power and control, but still alive and feeling a lot better about myself.

That is the way I hoped I could lead the rest of my life: so completely involved in things I valued, that I would not notice when the day I was supposed to die came and went. That is what is meant by "a good death," living a full life until the end.

A voice spoke to me out of the blue. I thought it was telling me when I would die. What it actually showed me was the way to live. It showed me that I was out of synchrony with myself and my environment, and that I should put things together. I thought it was saying "get your affairs in order, you are about to die"; it was actually saying "get yourself together, you are about to live."

Technically speaking I experienced a hallucination, but that seems unimportant. Whose voice was it? God's? Mine? My brother's? The voice of the universe? I do not know, but the boundaries implied by words like "universe" and "God" make me uneasy about using them. Maybe they are all clumsy human attempts to define what is beyond our comprehension.

The name "God" is used in too many specific ways by people believing different things for me to know what will be understood by using it. "Universe" also seems almost too broad and nonspecific for my comfort. Even "mine" or "my brother's" are terms that sometimes trouble me, for they often seem to overlap and extend either too far or not far enough. So choose any or all of them as the source of my voice, and I will not be offended.

It was not a voice that I recognized, but I like the idea that it was from the universe saying "Ouch" and telling me that the way I was leading my life was creating disharmony. I know that my universe is but an infinitesimal part of the larger universe; however, I do believe that mine and the larger one are connected. Since I know I can feel discomfort coming from some other part of the universe, when something happens out there that affects me, it may not be too farfetched to imagine that disharmony in me would also register elsewhere.

I assumed that I was being informed of the imminence of death. Changes were effected by this information, but when my will to maintain them faded, the voice spoke to remind me again. I could no longer ignore a message that seemed to tell me that my death was near. I had to acknowledge that there was not much time left, and so what remained was precious. I had to live in earnest, fully and with authenticity.

If the message had simply and directly been "you must live fully and with authenticity," I could easily have ignored it. The voice I heard was much wiser, and let me think death was imminent, a message that could not be taken lightly. Pointing the way without being explicit is often the more powerful way.

Ecclesiastes tells us there is a time for all things. I am grateful to my voice for shocking me into the realization that I was out of symmetry with my needs and my phase of life. That gave me a new opportunity to live as I believed I should. Thoreau's "As if you could kill time without injuring eternity" could have well applied to me. My voice showed me it was time to give up the obsolete in my life and do what was meaningful.

There are tasks associated with each phase of life. We are born and have to accept being cared for, we must grow and become more independent. We need to learn the skills of work and play, of effort and rest, of reaching out and closing up. We must learn to make our way in the world and then to care for others.

Towards the end we need to secure our place in the scheme of things by accepting what has been and what is now; by forgiving and finishing what is past; by consolidating the present and remaining open to the unknown future. Each season has its own usefulness and its own source of vitality.

And that applies to death as well. The disharmony of which that voice spoke was in how I was living my life, not with all of living, and so I am still here and gladly so. I can only hope that when it is really time to die that I will know, and yield with grace. I want to follow the principle of Seneca: "The wise man should live as long as he ought, not as long as he can."

TEN

Misery and Memory

I am very fond of truth, but not at all of martyrdom.

VOLTAIRE, *Letters to d'Alembert*

THE MISERY of being sick is quickly erased from the mind when one is well. When you first recover after an illness, the world seems a wonderland, and you are very grateful that you are still alive. You have great joy in the simplest movement of your body and in various things you hardly notice at other times.

But after a few days the magic sadly fades. Fortunately, though, what fades with it is the memory of just how miserable you were when you were sick. It was wise of nature to make us that way. Otherwise we would probably remain frozen in a continuous posture of fear. Memory loss is very convenient, and allows us the courage to go on.

It is probably an evolutionary development to forget such things. Those who could forget the terrible things that had happened to them were more likely to survive. They would not lose courage when faced with new adversity, for they had mercifully forgotten the terror associated with the past event.

Healthy people who have been able to forget how unpleasant an illness was may remember only certain, rather appealing aspects of the experience in retrospect. When they think of getting sick again, they may even think how nice it would be to get away from the "rat race" and go to a hospital where all of their needs would be taken care of.

When you talk to people who are still in the hospital and still in the midst of feeling bad, it's a very different story. They feel miserable, and all that keeps them going is the hope and promise that things will soon be different, and they can be back to doing what they like.

Anyone who has ever been seasick knows how all-consuming illness can be: "You think you might die, and are afraid you *won't.*" Still, most people remember how much they enjoyed a sea voyage, and the memory of the sick feeling is less intense. Although admittedly seasickness gives a person a particularly acute feeling of being sick, it illustrates the more general problem as well.

It also illustrates how helpless you feel. Is anyone who is seasick ever noble or courageous? You are reduced to the most primitive level on the evolutionary scale, caring about nothing but yourself, and then only about getting your misery to stop.

But when you are healthy and feeling well again, that all seems very remote and unfamiliar. That is one reason the able-bodied and healthy often have so little sympathy with the sick and disabled. It is very hard to identify with them.

As a doctor, before I was disabled I found much of what my patients experienced to be incomprehensible. I tried to be sympathetic, as much as most people did; however, what was happening to them was outside of my own experience. I was strong and athletic. Whatever illnesses I had were usually short-lived and I quickly forgot their unpleasantness. Moreover, I was developing the doctor's necessary insulation from too much feeling—too much can be incapacitating.

I believe I appeared quite sympathetic, and I tried hard to be, because I thought it was the right thing to do. But there was little depth to my feelings. I was "play acting," as people do when going through the motions of showing concern. How often do people inquire about another's health without really noticing or caring what they say? Just let someone take such an inquiry seriously, and you will see how quickly the subject is changed. If it is not, then the person will be labeled a bore or a hypochondriac in the future.

So I used to wonder at how profoundly my patients were troubled by their being sick. I believed that I would be more stoic and untroubled than they. That may well have been true, for I had never been sick long enough for the erosion of spirit to become solidified. For the short term, being strong and courageous is not so difficult.

History memorializes Nathan Hale and other heroes whose brave resistance remained stalwart even when they were held captive and tortured by overwhelmingly powerful adversaries. Such examples serve the purposes of society by encouraging its members to resist foreign invaders. However, these examples are usually drawn from patriots who made a single dramatic demonstration of courage.

Admirable as they are, the pressures they had to endure were not prolonged. In other cases, although confined for an extended period, they continued to have evidence of support from the outside, and mistreatment was attenuated.

But when there is no hope of release, the strength to resist slowly fades. There is a limit to the capacity of the human mind and spirit to overcome and compensate for a ravaged body. People imprisoned in times of war or political oppression can hold out and remain courageous for a time, but with sufficient cruelty and torture, sooner or later anyone can be broken. Those who imprison and preside over the erosion of their captive's will know that time is on their side. The relentless pressure gradually wears the victim down and reduces him to a primitive level. With his strength gone, all that remains is a cowering animal who can think of little besides escaping the agony. Any more elevated thoughts are forgotten.

Of course there are important differences between prisoners and patients. Patients are ordinarily not subjected to deliberate cruelty, and they have the advantage of clean quarters. However, in many ways it is even harder for a patient to remain resolute than for a prisoner.

A political prisoner or a captive of war is imprisoned because of his beliefs. If he holds them strongly, they may serve him well by giving meaning and purpose to his discomfort. By contrast, a patient's misery seems without purpose. His suffering seems meaningless and does no good, and no one he knows will benefit from it, especially not himself.

Moreover, the prisoner knows who the enemy is. He can focus all of his efforts on resisting that enemy, further helping him to remain strong and courageous. Both prisoners and patients will benefit from knowing that there are people outside who support them, but it is easier if they also know clearly who the enemy is.

The patient's only enemy is the part of himself which is ill. So he must struggle against himself, and he is all alone in doing so. If he is in a hospital, most of the people around him are carefully objective and neutral. No one is against him, some staff may be supportive, but most are neutral and just doing their jobs.

In California, a young woman named Elizabeth Bouvia recently attracted considerable media attention when she petitioned the court to allow her to die. She was born with severe cerebral palsy, making speech and movement nearly impossible. Through years of arduous effort she gradually learned to speak, although not clearly. A wheelchair made it possible for her to be moved about.

She displayed great courage in trying to lead a "normal" life. She attended college, and eventually received a master's degree and became a social worker. She later married, and kept house for her husband. Every movement and every word she uttered continued to require enormous effort. In spite of these severe disabilities, she had done everything within her power to overcome them.

After a time, partly due to the strains she had placed on her body, she developed a painfully incapacitating arthritis. Her marriage failed, and she was ultimately divorced. No longer employable, she was in continuous pain and lay bedridden in a hospital. Then all pain medication was withheld from her because of fear that she was becoming addicted.

She was alone, without resources, in constant pain, confined to a hospital, and without substantial hope of improvement. Because she was unable to move from her bed, there was no way in which she could take her own life. So she petitioned the court to help her to die.

There was an outpouring of media coverage, and it nearly all maligned the poor woman. The reactions were in essence "how dare she affront society by this request?" She was called manipulative, publicity-seeking, and malicious.

The "right to life" organizations objected on religious and moral grounds. "Human rights" groups feared that to grant her wish would open the door to death camps for those who are different, raising the specter of the Holocaust.

Even advocates for the disabled complained that her request might suggest that all disabled people wanted to die, or feared that the disabled would be branded as cowards. And then, threatened medical authorities reassured the public that pain could safely and easily be controlled, and since the comfort of their patients was always uppermost in their minds, no one need suffer.

I have never met Ms. Bouvia, so I do not know if her critics' accusations were true, but what surprised me was that her request was not seriously addressed. Instead, she was maligned in such a way that would support the particular cause of each spokesperson. The very personal plight of poor Ms. Bouvia was lost in the ideological polemics, and it was she, and she alone, who had to live this way.

I do not question the sincerity of those who spoke out, nor do I doubt that their causes have a great deal of merit. But the real tragedy is that the fate of this one human being was completely out of her hands, and had become a matter for public policy debate.

The people who ignore the person in favor of the cause that interests them must never have experienced, or have conveniently forgotten, what pain, incapacity, and hospitalization are like. Having survived intact from whatever limited personal encounters they have had with illness, they are free of its intimidating effects. So they doubt the sincerity of someone like Ms. Bouvia, and erroneously assume that she is acting hysterically.

But what they cannot imagine is the eroding effects of the continuous struggle, without respite. That is the least understood and most overwhelming part of the problem. When everything you have to do requires effort, the will is slowly drained until nothing remains, and the only hope is in the peace of death. Each movement, each word spoken, each activity undertaken, must have required Herculean effort for Ms. Bouvia, and in the end she was not only without tangible reward, but without the will to go on. Just as the joints of her body had become worn out, so too was her spirit broken.

Hard work for good purpose is not necessarily rewarded by earthly success; usually it is not. The only assured reward that one can count on is that the effort was in a good cause; "no athlete is crowned but in the sweat on his brow." But that intangible reward had grown thin for Ms. Bouvia, and who am I to say that it should have been enough for her? It is she, and she alone, who must live in her body, and if any of us wish to assume responsibility for how she wishes to do that, should we not also be required to suffer her agony?

What could be any more devastating than life without meaningful purpose? Although no one can ever completely deny recovery as a possibility, Ms. Bouvia, according to reports, could not reasonably expect improvement. Certainly the chances were extremely remote. Moreover, she was young, and could expect to live for many more hopeless years.

Perhaps there are some people who in similar circumstances could find some meaning in life, but the important point is that Ms. Bouvia could not, and it was she who had to face each day. To look forward only to useless years of existence must be the cruelest torture of all.

Ms. Bouvia was given what for her was a far worse punishment than a death sentence; she was given a life sentence to serve a life devoid of meaning. She could not envision an alternative, even if one had been offered to her. How many others who cannot envision any viable alternative are suffering similar life sentences without meaning, and should they be forced to continue to do so?

Ms. Bouvia saw the world through the darkest of windows. For her there was no other window. Should she and those in similar situations be forced to live in agony because I or someone else believes that a brighter view exists? Those of us who think there is one are then obliged to show its presence to them. Otherwise, by what authority do we control that they should live or die?

From all reports Ms. Bouvia does not now live in grace. The question for her, and eventually for each of us as well, is, in death can grace yet be restored?

ELEVEN

My Mother

I have no regrets. I have done the best I could.

My mother

M Y MOTHER does not know how old she is. We think she is somewhere between eighty-eight and ninety-two years old. She says it does not matter, and she does not care.

She has lived a hard life, but she is a survivor. She has buried two husbands and her eldest son—and I, her only other child, have been paralyzed most of my life. It has not been easy for her.

She has lived by serving others and doing what she had to do, uncomplaining and generous always. Even in the darkest times she has done her job, and more.

It is very hard for her to walk now, and she had to give up driving several years ago when her eyesight failed. She now lives alone, tries to keep house herself, and until recently went to the senior citizens center to play bridge occasionally. She usually spends a few days each week with us.

She not only lives alone, she feels alone. When she had the strength, she worked as a volunteer at the senior center, the library, and Meals on Wheels. She does not like taking care of no one but herself, yet she is not up to doing any more. In fact, she is not able to do a very good job of taking care of herself. She now forgets to eat sometimes, and cannot seem to keep her pills straight or remember when she is supposed to take them.

She once had lots of friends, but only two are still alive, and they are both in nursing homes, requiring full-time care. She played bridge in the same group of eight for sixty years. Now she is the only one left. At the senior center she made new friends, some very dear, but they too are now gone. She does not seem to have the heart or strength to try again.

I call her every day by phone, but our conversation, once full of excitement and exchange, has now dried up. There is not much to say. Not much is going on for her, and her attention lags when I tell her of my day. She has heard it all before, I fear.

Because she lives fifty miles away, we have wanted her to move in with us, or at least nearer. If she did, we could take her places, and give her more support in other ways as well. She sometimes says she will, but after a day or two with us insists on going home.

When she stays with us, everything is strange: she cannot work the stove, the thermostats, or the telephones, much less the VCR, the TV remote control, and the telephone answering machine. She becomes confused, and cannot wait until she can get back to her familiar home.

She says she does not want to leave her home, the place where she belongs. It is her home, and has been for a very long time. There she feels secure. Secure, but lonely. But we do not feel secure about her.

I am worried. She is fragile, and what if she should fall? What if there were a fire or a burglary? What if she could not reach the telephone, and she needed help?

My cousin from the East visited my mother, and told me simply that I had to move her to a more secure environment! Even against her will. She too was worried about my mother's safety, and she said that if my mother could not see a move was right, then I had to do it anyhow.

I talked with my mother, and told her our concern again. She said she did not want to be a worry to me, so if I would be relieved, she would move. I know how much she hates to burden others, so I know she meant it. She made it clear, just the same, that for herself alone, she would not leave her home.

So we decided to try another way—to have someone live with my mother in her home. She met with several people. The first complained that my mother's appliances, the ones that she can work, were too old and should be replaced. The second had her own furniture, which she wanted to have in place of my mother's. The third, my mother said, needed more help than she did.

On her next visit to us, in spite of her resistance, we decided to visit retirement homes. I called some friends who had been through similar problems with their parents. They generously shared their own experiences, but none seemed to have been very satisfactory. So we looked in the yellow pages.

The first on our list was the one nearest to our home. We live in a lovely residential community, so we thought we could not go too far wrong in visiting.

From the outside it looked like an apartment house of moderate means. There was no yard. Inside it was unmistakably an institution—long hallways with regimented furnishings. There were bulletin boards on either side of the entry: one showed weekly menus, the other, weekly activities. Behind a glass enclosure a serious-looking woman sat behind a desk.

There was a subtle but pervasive odor that I have since come to associate with many such facilities—staleness, not pungent but definite. And then there were the residents. They sat in rows, some reading, some watching TV, but most just staring. Of the fifty or so people in the "dayrooms," I saw none in conversation, and I saw none in motion. No one smiled or looked up at our intrusion.

We spoke to the woman in the office and got her sales pitch, much of it about money and "professionalism." Although the home accepted only ambulatory people who could care for themselves, one of the big advantages there, she said, was that when the residents required full-time nursing care, they could simply move next door to the adjoining nursing home.

I noticed while we talked that no one had come to the office for anything. They continued in whatever isolated activity they had been engaged.

My mother was becoming agitated. So was I. She said, "No one smiles," and let me know that she wanted to leave, right now.

My wife took her out to the car, but I decided, despite my own discomfort, to stay a little longer. I approached one of the residents, selecting the one I thought most likely to be open—a pleasant-looking octogenarian woman who was knitting.

I told her what I was doing there, and asked her opinion about the place. "It's okay," she said, with an inflection, implying "what do you expect?" I asked about the quarters, the personnel, the food, the activities. All of her responses were much the same—without interest or enthusiasm, no condemnation, just apathy. As I left she volunteered, "It isn't home."

There were about four women to every man. I approached a couple of others, one man, one woman. Their verbal responses were similarly noncommittal and apathetic. The man bitterly wanted me to know that he would not be there except that his son wanted to get rid of him. The woman did not seem to care.

I felt hopeless and depressed, and I certainly could not think of having my mother stay here. I did think I had better look around at the rest of the place, just to familiarize myself more.

I saw a couple of the rooms. They were not too bad, but far from what she would like, I thought. Then I asked to see the nursing care facility next door. That is when I really got depressed.

Half of the people were in beds, the other half tied into wheelchairs. Tiny shriveled caricatures of what they once had been, they stared ahead with unseeing eyes, locked in some forgotten place.

Occasionally a nurse's aide would lean over to do something to or for one of them, but it seemed to be done without human contact. Not that there was not "honey" this or "honey" that, but nothing I saw of real exchange.

Punctuating the whole macabre scene were groans and other subhuman sounds coming from some of their half-open parchment mouths, groans unrelated to any activity I could see. Were they in pain? Or reliving something from the past? We will never know.

The words of Edwin Markham's *The Man with the Hoe* kept going through my mind:

> Bowed by the weight of centuries he leans
> Upon his hoe and gazes on the ground,
> The emptiness of ages in his face,
> And on his back the burden of the world.
> Who made him dead to rapture and despair,
> A thing that grieves not and that never hopes,
> Stolid and stunned, a brother to the ox?
> Who loosened and let down this brutal jaw?
> Whose was the hand that slanted back this brow?
> Whose breath blew out the light within this brain?
>
> Is this the Thing the Lord God made and gave
> To have dominion over sea and land;

To trace the stars and search the heavens for power;
To feel the passion of Eternity?
Is this the Dream He dreamed who shaped the suns
And marked their ways upon the ancient deep?
Down all the stretch of Hell to its last gulf
There is no shape more terrible than this—
More tongued with censure of the world's blind greed—
More filled with signs and portents for the soul—
More fraught with menace to the universe.

Although originally the poem was designed to show the tragedy of exploited laborers, Markham's description now fits the plight of the elderly in custodial institutions.

When I returned to the car, where my mother was waiting with my wife, there was a real sense of despair. My mother could not get over the fact that no one smiled. She said she was tired, wanted to go home, and needed to rest.

The next day she was sullen, unlike herself. When I approached the subject, she reacted testily: "I am not going to one of those places." I tried to say that this was only one retirement facility, and there were many different kinds and many different qualities of them. I said I would like to see others before we came to a final decision.

She continued, uncharacteristically adamant, "I have always taken care of myself [indeed she had done that, and cared for others as well], and as long as I am responsible, I will continue to do so."

I told her again of my concern for her safety. She reminded me that I had made my concern clear before. She said, "I have lived my life. I am not afraid to die. I am ready, and have been. But I don't want to be dead while I am still alive, and that's what would happen to me if I went to one of those places."

The place we had gone to was considered to be well above the average. But I was determined to see the very best alternatives. My wife and I began to visit the most promising ones.

I found the most expensive retirement facility in an elegant high rise on the oceanfront. Inside and out it appeared similar to a fine resort hotel. The public rooms were cheerfully appointed, and had ocean views. The private rooms were also spacious and fairly attractive.

The sales pitch was much slicker and designed for snob appeal. But all the time I listened, I was aware of that characteristic odor that I had smelled. Smell is fundamental to all emotion, and whatever trappings might be used to conceal what is basic, in smell it may be revealed. As posh as it looked, this place was still a human warehouse.

After the formal tour I asked to be allowed to talk to some of the residents. It took considerable huddling and whispering before permission was granted.

The residents here were more stylishly dressed, still only a handful of men to many women. Even so, most sat staring vacantly. A few seemed to have private paid companions that sat quietly with them.

I found a couple of women who were talking in one

corner. I approached them and told them of my mission. Did they like it here? I asked. There was no immediate response. Then: "Well, if you have to be someplace . . ." said one, trailing off. "I'm going back to Chicago," the other said. "This is not where I live; I just exist."

I asked about the various details of living, and got the same kind of apathetic answers as at the first place. I explained my dilemma about my mother, and that did get a response: "Tell your mother to stay in her own home as long as she can."

These were or had been very capable women. They were well-to-do. They were here because they had to be, but they did not like it. I could see their dissatisfaction did not have to do with the quality of the facility, but with feeling old and useless.

Between us, my wife and I visited several more facilities and interviewed twenty-five or thirty more residents. Their comments were much the same as those I have described. I did speak to a married couple in one place who seemed genuinely content. There were a few others who accepted their situation, with mild reservations. Some seemed to be comfortable, but at the cost of considerable dementia. I am sure there are others who have found a satisfying home in a retirement facility, but they are probably a minority.

I did not ask, nor did I feel I could ask, the crucial question: "Is living here so bad that you would rather be dead?" Anyhow, most people do not think of death as a viable [*sic*] option, so I doubt that I could get much beyond a social response.

For her part, my mother says she is ready to die. I try to show her that there can be another window from which to see, that she is loved and is of value to us now. She always says something like "Thank you, I know you want the best for me," but remains unmoved. I tell her that although things seem hopeless now, with our help she will see that the world is alive for her again.

My friend Jerry thoughtfully suggested that perhaps she indeed is ready to die, and that my job may be to release her so she can leave in peace and without guilt. I can see the wisdom there, and I do want her life to be her own, with whatever support she needs to keep it so.

She called me the other day and said, "I just can't manage; you will have to take over." We brought her to our home, saw that she ate, straightened out her medication schedule, and saw that her needs were met. There is also activity here, and she is involved when visitors come by. In a few days she was feeling better. Then she began to insist on going home.

This has happened several times before, so I tried to remind her that she is better when with us. She told me that I did not understand. "At home I can be myself, and don't have to depend on anyone. I know how everything works, and I am in control. I have taken care of myself all my life, and it is my life, and I am responsible for it. You are not."

She is right, I understand only to a point. I think that if

she is stronger here, more alert and less depressed, this is where she should be. For her, those things are less important than being responsible for herself alone. She is right, for it is her life.

In earlier times people probably would not have lived so long, but my mother has had the best in modern medical care. She does have diabetes and circulatory insufficiency, and has had heart failure on a few occasions. Skillful care has stabilized her each time. She has a caring social worker from the local hospital, who visits each week. She also has support from several other community agencies. Still, she feels she has lost all usefulness and purpose, and is just waiting to die.

I am well aware that my mother's situation is better than it would be for most people of her age and state of health. In some respects my mother represents the best of this bad situation. But before modern health care, people would not have lived so long, and when they did, support without physical dislocation would probably have been possible from an extended family.

Aldous Huxley anticipated the growth of an older population living beyond its usefulness. He wrote in *Brave New World* that a standardized means of death kept the population of older people down. Everyone was genetically programmed to develop "galloping senility," which led rapidly and painlessly to death at age sixty-five.

I hope we never come to anything like that, but it may be a real danger unless we can find some better ways of supporting people in their personal choices to live or die.

The unhappiness of these elderly people is hardly a just conclusion to their lives.

Perhaps if we can find adequate means to allow the elderly to live in dignity until they die naturally, there will be no need to consider the fearful alternatives. But the likelihood of that seems diminishingly small, considering the combination of pressures: financial, legal, medical, and religious, all well meaning.

And if the problem is to continue and grow worse, should we not cautiously consider death by choice another option? It is not an option now for most people because of the shame and stigma attached to it. Could it not, if chosen freely, become a rite of passage that would include the loving support of family and friends? This could become a celebration of a life well lived, a fitting culmination of grace and dignity, and a demonstration to all of the continuity of life from generation to generation.

TWELVE

Jesus and Socrates

So our lives
In acts exemplary, not only win
Ourselves good names, but doth to others give
Matter for virtuous deeds, by which we live.

GEORGE CHAPMAN, *Bussy d'Ambois*

JESUS AND SOCRATES are dominant figures in the spiritual and intellectual life of Western civilization. Yet neither left any personal texts, and all that we know about them and their ideas comes from the writings of their followers and students. The legacy of Socrates is rationality and critical thought, and it supports the development of the science and technology of today. Jesus' life and works were dedicated to faith and love, and led to the development of the foremost religious orientation in the West today.

Each was persecuted, tried, and martyred for his beliefs and commitments. Yet in spite of the judgments rendered and carried out by the authorities of the times, for two millennia afterward, their lives and ideas have continued to serve as inspiration and guidance for those seeking a better world.

The life of Jesus of Nazareth hardly needs repeating, for it is an essential element in Christian beliefs, and the most widely known story in Western civilization. His death was a human tragedy, even though it became a great spiritual triumph. Jesus' life on earth was very short, for he was only about thirty-three years old at the time of his death.

He held beliefs that were alien to his people and criminal in the eyes of their conquerors. His most ardent and loyal supporters left him at the time of his greatest need for them. Because he declared himself "the son of God," his tormentors placed a crown of thorns upon his head. He was mocked, and forced to carry the burden of the very cross on which he was to be crucified. On the cross he was hung by nails driven through his flesh, and left to suffer there until death mercifully freed him.

There are similarities between the earthly fate of Jesus and that of Socrates. There are also important differences. Socrates was the great Athenian philosopher who lived during the golden age of Pericles. He was known as the teacher of many of the other famous philosophers of that period. He taught rigorous thinking by challenging and questioning the acceptance of traditional beliefs. To stimulate the thinking of his disciples, he employed what we now call the "Socratic method." Only rarely did he openly declare his own conclusions, but instead led his students to reach their own, which were not necessarily consistent with his.

Later, when some of his former students began to challenge the existing order, threatened officials erroneously suspected that Socrates was responsible for their actions. He was charged in vague terms with the criminal behavior of "corruption of the young" and "neglect of the gods." But despite his innocence, Socrates refused to take any action to clear his good name. The only defense he was willing to offer was a further avowal and justification of his teaching.

Since he was unrepentant, the court found him guilty and, according to the law of the time, sentenced him to death. Because of his prominence, however, he was assured that if he would only stop teaching, his sentence would be commuted. When he refused, he was even given the opportunity of making a counterproposal. Banishment, for example, would have been acceptable.

Even after he was convicted, his students and followers did not desert him, and instead planned an escape for him. But Socrates insisted that the verdict was that of a legitimate court, and so should be obeyed.

Socrates, like Jesus, remained steadfast to the end, and would not consider giving up his convictions. He would accept only a judgment of guilty or an acquittal—anything less would be self-betrayal in his view.

While in prison, he continued to live as he always had. He was surrounded by friends and disciples and he continued to involve them in stimulating dialogues. They were true to him to the end, and he remained faithful to his vocation. The story of his last day, in the company of his friends and students, is memorialized in the *Phaedo* by Plato, who was one of them.

It was in these circumstances, at age seventy, that Socrates drank the poisonous hemlock in 399 B.C. He was a martyr for his beliefs. His choice had been between an uncompromised death or remaining alive without the freedom to teach his students in the manner of his beliefs. He unhesitatingly chose the hemlock rather than life without purpose for him: death with meaning, rather than meaningless life.

Socrates had a "good death," just as he had a "good life." He had lived his life fully. He died true to his convictions, surrounded by those he loved and who loved him. When he drank the hemlock, he died quickly and painlessly. So he was a martyr to his cause, but a martyr without suffering. It is hardly possible to conceive of better circumstances under which to die.

Roman justice at the time of Jesus was not as humane as the earlier Athenian system had been. Jesus was forced to experience the most excruciating of deaths—crucifixion. Exposed to the elements, nailed to the cross, he died an agonizingly slow and painful death.

Socrates had the good fortune to be surrounded by those who were dear to him. But Jesus was forsaken and betrayed by those he loved. Alone, deserted, and in the most terrible pain, he died a death which could easily have been forgotten but for the fact that it was filled with the most profound of spiritual meanings to Jesus and all who have followed him. It was not a "good death" in the temporal sense that Socrates' was, although it was a most momentous and inspiring religious event.

Both men could have saved themselves from death if only they had been willing to recant and give up teaching their ideas. The price was too high, though. Each unhesitatingly refused to do so, and we have admired them for their courage ever since. In bidding farewell to their followers, without concession, each was assured of a place in history and achieved a form of immortality that *is* available to human beings.

They both could have continued to live, but it would have been life without meaning. It would have been a life in which they had to deny a vital part of themselves, their very purpose in living. If they had given in, they would then have been no more than hollow men without substance. That would have been a far worse fate for them—it would have been a living death.

Socrates was an old man; Jesus was young. Socrates was surrounded by those he loved; Jesus was alone. Socrates died quickly without pain; Jesus died slowly in agony. Although Socrates had a good death and Jesus suffered a terrible one, both accepted their fates willingly, because the alternative was to give up what gave meaning to their lives. Their lives on earth were less important to them than what they believed. The critical element was what in contemporary terminology we call the "quality of life."

Reverence for life is a fundamental value for me, and I share with "right to life" advocates a belief in the sanctity of all life. Often, however, they seem to overlook that Jesus could have saved his biological life by abandoning the meaning and quality of his mental and spiritual life.

Such a choice can never be easy for one who values life and respects what is often referred to as God's will. Not wishing to interfere with or violate the sanctity of the forces of the universe, one must have doubts about making life-and-death choices, even if they are only of personal concern. Some would like to reduce the question to a choice between God's will or man's will.

But how can we ever be certain of what God's will is? We have already interfered with nature in so many different ways, that what is natural—what is "God's will"—is very difficult to discern. Even the concept of "natural" can only be hypothetical, for the very existence of man effects change in the environment.

In societies where there has been limited human interference in the natural order, most people die before they reach forty years of age. Death is usually swift and violent, so suffering is brief. These people do not face the same problems of lingering death that have been created by the successes of modern medicine. Few of the sick or injured could languish very long without the supportive medical intervention that now keeps people alive. Since it is we who keep the suffering alive, it is also we who are in a position to liberate them.

If Jesus had been given a choice between the agonizing death he suffered and a "good" one like Socrates had, which would he have chosen? Perhaps he would have chosen hemlock over crucifixion, if nothing of his beliefs would be lost, and if there were no good purpose served by suffering. Perhaps he would have preferred to be surrounded by friends, too.

There can certainly be value in suffering for a good cause, and if someone can see meaning in it, he deserves our admiration. But what if, in the eyes of the person involved, no good purpose is served? Tragically, that is the case for most who exist in torment in contemporary hospitals and convalescent facilities. They are not suffering for a cause, and there is no meaning in their pain.

Would a loving god, like the one Jesus knew, want meaningless suffering? Would he want meaningless life? I think not. Some say that no one should have the right to choose between life or death for himself. Perhaps the people who make such claims might be able to find meaning in life under most any conditions. But can one person know if there is meaning in another's life better than the subject himself? Those who believe in that kind of authority are moving dangerously close to providing justification for the actions of those who martyred Jesus and Socrates.

When I was young, I rarely thought about death and when I did, it seemed very remote. I certainly was not concerned about my own death. I thought about it in the fourth grade when Lucille died, and again in the seventh grade when Lyle did. Then there is the poignant and personally prophetic statement in my high school yearbook that "we were all saddened when Galen Rand died of polio."

In my mind they all seemed different from me, fundamentally flawed in some way—otherwise they would not have died, I thought at the time. I had a lot to overcome to arrive at that conclusion in Lyle's case, because he had been a very good friend. He was witty and just as athletic as I.

When I got polio and was completely paralyzed, I certainly thought a lot about death. I was afraid of dying when I was first sick, and still thought I might recover completely. When I could see that I was not going to improve, I wanted to be dead. Otherwise it looked like my life would be without meaning—no sports, no being a doctor, no activities of the kind I had been accustomed to and loved.

When I was first sick and hovered between life and death, I was surrounded by loved ones. Family and friends served a constant vigil for weeks. Visitors came from opposite sides of the country (even though I could not see most) and I got hundreds of telegrams, letters, and calls. It would have been a *good death* in many respects, even though premature.

Then, much of the support gradually began to fade for, after all, how long can people maintain hope and continue to disrupt their own lives? When it was clear that I would not recover, many gave up and left. Many realized that I would not be the same person again, and could see that it would be like meeting someone new. Some felt embarrassed and awkward about my disability.

I felt hurt and deserted at the time. Although, in retrospect, if I had not felt so ashamed and awkward about myself, I could have done a great deal to make it easier for many people to continue as friends. I had lost most of what had given my life meaning, part of which had been these relationships. I was helpless and without hope.

I wanted to be dead, but I could find no possible way of taking my life, since I could not move. I had no choice; I was forced to live, and now I am very glad I did, because it became a good life. There were many years, though, when it seemed very grim. If my life had ended during one of those times, it would have been without regret on my part.

I did have youth on my side, and over the years I was gradually able, with the help of many old and many new friends, to develop a new life with new and often very different meanings in it. The important thing is that it came to have—and much of the time now continues to have—meaning for me, and as long as it does, I hope to live.

Because I am now what is euphemistically called a senior citizen, and death is no longer so remote, many of my contemporaries and I often speak of it. Every time the subject comes up, someone is sure to express the hope that when it is time, they and their loved ones will die quickly and painlessly, while their faculties are still intact.

The great fears they express are of pain, hospitalization, institutionalization, and loss of faculties. This is the case whether they're speaking of parents, spouses, or themselves, and whether they are Protestant, Catholic, Jewish, or something else. Although there are often differences in how they would plan to handle the situation, their fears remain the same. The universal threat is the extended, painful, meaningless life—not the death of the body.

There have been times in my life when I had no useful function, except perhaps the employment of people to take care of me. These have been times of mental anguish and spiritual deadness, even though my body was still alive.

Fortunately, although some of these periods lasted as long as three years when I first became ill, they were not permanent. But now my capacity for recovery has diminished. Soon there will come a time when recovery to any functional degree will no longer be a possibility, and I will no longer be able to be or do what has useful meaning for me. I hope I will not have to linger very long then.

To be concerned about such matters is very self-centered, and only possible because I live in a land of opportunity at a time of plenty. There is no opportunity for reflections of this nature when people live under constant threat of famine, pestilence, war, or similar emergency. The instinct for survival takes precedence over any concern about quality of life then, and indeed the majority of people in this world do exist in such hazardous circumstances.

But that is precisely why we, who are so blessed, need to reconsider the allocation of resources. For increasing amounts of the world's resources are being used to warehouse the elderly and infirm of the developed nations, maintaining them in woeful circumstances that are satisfying to no one. At the same time millions of young people elsewhere are deprived of the barest opportunity to express their potential, because they live in desperate economic conditions without resources.

Much is spent on keeping people biologically alive who are spiritually and mentally lifeless, and who would prefer deliverance. No one who wants his life to continue and can find any useful meaning in it should ever have it taken from him. But for those whose physical, mental, and spiritual resources have been spent, and who see no purpose in continuing in agony, we need a way to release them with dignity and support in accordance with their wishes. We must seek new ways to express the faith and compassion of Jesus with the rationality and reason of Socrates.

True reverence for life includes all life, not just that of any single individual. And all life must share the common fate on earth of death. If we can reserve at least a part of who we are for the whole of life, individual death is not so overwhelming.

THIRTEEN

Difference in Life and Death

It ain't over 'til it's over.

YOGI BERRA

EVERYONE KNOWS that there is a difference between life and death; it is self-evident. But only in this era of science and medical technology has it become a matter of legal definition and public policy debate.

Among the ancients, when someone stopped moving for a time, that was enough; he was considered to be dead. Even if he still had life within him, it made little difference. If he could not move, he could not care for himself; he would die very soon anyway. So he might as well be considered dead.

Along came magicians of various kinds, and ultimately doctors as we know them today. They were able to affect some people in ways that could keep them from dying, or they could artificially resuscitate them. That complicated matters considerably. So a search to find more reliable indicators of life began.

One of the early methods focused on breathing. Breath was thought to be the essence of life as well as the seat of the soul, *prana* to the Hindus. If the person was breathing, he must be alive; if not, he must be dead.

To determine if someone was alive, people would look for evidence in movements of the chest, or they would listen for breath sounds. And in what must have been one of the earliest attempts at technology, they would hold a mirror or other shiny object next to the person's nose and mouth to see if condensation would appear.

As people grew more sophisticated, they realized that although the breath might stop, the heartbeat could continue to support life. So they felt for pulsations in arteries and in the chest. The heart seemed to be the source of life, and this gave rise to concepts such as "courage"—from *cuer,* meaning the heart.

Then the brain, as the organ of the mind, came into prominence. It became recognized that the functions of seeing, hearing, and each of the other senses depended on the integrity of specific areas of the brain. The same was true of the abilities to speak, understand, reason, and think —all of consciousness. Malfunctions in any or all of these systems occurred when the brain was damaged.

Gradually crude evidences of brain activity were refined through the use of neurological tests and electroencephalograms for charting brain waves. We now have learned that although the heart and lungs may continue to function, a person may be "brain-dead." When a person's brain shows no evidence of electrochemical activity, we can assume it has ceased to function; there being no recorded case of recovery from that state, it is safe to say that his brain is indeed dead. Most people would agree that although the rest of his body may be kept medically alive, he has permanently ceased to function as a human being.

Perhaps the most famous case of this kind was that of Karen Ann Quinlan, a tragic young woman who was kept alive for many years while she was brain-dead. Her family ultimately obtained a legal judgment, so her body would be able to rejoin her mind and spirit in death. But it did not happen without wrenching and publicized medical and legal proceedings that stripped the process of all privacy and dignity.

Today we have other technological advances that produce an even more complex picture. We can transplant the organs of one person to another to maintain life. The heart, the lungs, the kidney, the skin, the cornea, and the liver of one person can restore functions in another, and operations for this purpose have become almost routine. Today nearly every other organ of the body, even the brain, is under study for future transplants.

Moreover, artificial means—machines—can breathe for a person, or provide kidney, heart, and other functions. Although they are admittedly not yet refined, we nevertheless even have electronic devices that can replace the functions of arms and legs, perhaps even spinal cords and brains. All of these developments further confuse an already confused situation.

The more we have learned about sustaining the body, the more complicated distinguishing life from death has become. We realize now that the various physiological functions can be maintained separately from one another, and similarly the mental and spiritual aspects of life can be independent of many of these.

If someone is brain-dead, most people would believe he no longer has functioning mental and spiritual activity. In less severe conditions a person may also be deprived of such capacities, and reduced to low levels of animal function.

We have already considered how torture, pain, discomfort, and weakness may produce such reductions in the human spirit so that there is no awareness of altruistic, moral, or ethical choices. All that remains is the reflex instinct to survive—not too different from the person who survives on medical life support machines, but is brain-dead. The ravages of age and disease produce the same results of biological life with spiritual death.

Since we can now continue many, perhaps most, biological functions for extended periods, but not necessarily at levels that would allow activity with a useful purpose, we must reexamine our reasons for doing so. What was perfectly rational when people were both clearly alive *and* able to choose how they lived becomes irrational when we can maintain their biological lives without their being able to make such choices.

We cannot allow ourselves to become so enamored with our scientific and technological advances that we forget what is more basic. We are in danger of being able to sustain biological life, while we forget why. In fact, that has already happened in the vast warehouses that contain the bodies of the elderly, who have life but have lost meaning. We are forced to face the most fundamental and the most difficult question: what is a person, and when does he cease being one?

When is a person a person? When is he alive? When is he dead? These have always been enormously complicated questions, and today, with each scientific and technological advance, they become more and more complex and problematic. Yet they are not merely conceptual issues, they also affect daily practical decisions of the highest order, especially at the extremes of life, at birth and death.

Whose rights must be considered—the individual's alone? The answer may probably be yes, but who indeed is the individual? A mother carrying a child before birth? The child? The father? And if the child, when? At birth? At viability? At conception? And what of those born without a brain and without evidence of any human awareness?

The problem has entered every sphere of life, and created the sad spectacle of confrontation between those who support a woman's rights and those who support a man's or a child's—sometimes resulting in violence. Nearly everyone has very strong feelings on the subject.

While it is the other end of life that is the concern here, the issues are related. The questions sound the same: when is a person still a person, when is he alive, and when is he more nearly dead?

Consider the case of a man or a woman who is completely paralyzed and cannot even speak, unable to do anything for himself or herself, and requiring nursing care around the clock. No layman or physician believes he or she can regain any of what has been lost; in fact, all agree that the condition is progressive, and inexorably will lead to death.

If the person is Stephen Hawking, one of the world's most distinguished mathematicians, then he is very much alive, and at the very pinnacle of his career. Now in his forties, he currently occupies the Cambridge University chair once held by Sir Isaac Newton. He is so alive, that to promote his bestselling book he has been on a strenuous travel and speaking schedule (since he cannot actually talk, his lectures are delivered by a speech synthesizer).

His life has meaning and significance to others and to himself. He has many friends and an active family life. Although his condition is progressive, it is very slowly so, and he is not in pain. His mind is not only unimpaired, but at the very peak of its acuity, and he is a great inspiration to all. He does not want to die, and he has work to do.

But what if he is a different person? Instead of being in his forties, he is in his eighties. He, like Hawking, cannot care for himself, but unlike the mathematician is indifferently cared for in a nursing home. His family and friends are gone, and he has no visitors. He has continuous discomfort and pain, and has become addicted to medications. He moans in pain whenever he is touched or moved. Each time a doctor visits him, he asks, "Please make me die."

Is he alive, or is this only the shell that once contained the man? Is there meaning in his life, and if so, to whom?

If he is still a person, the only wish that he expresses is to die.

And if his kidneys fail, should dialysis be done? And if he stops eating, will tube feedings be used to maintain his body? When his breathing ceases, will a tracheotomy and respirator be used to keep him alive?

What if he left no living will, no durable power of attorney? If his friends and family are gone, and he can no longer speak for himself, there will be no one to speak for the man that used to be. Is he still more alive than dead? And there are also lots of cases, as in Alzheimer's disease, wherein the body remains intact, with the mind and spirit nearly gone. What of them?

Hawking's body barely remains alive, but his mind and spirit are in full flower. The other man's body barely lives, and the main evidences of mind and spirit come from hearing his cries of pain. With Alzheimer's disease, the body may function, and the mind almost not at all.

So the differences between life and death are such arbitrary "calls" that they cannot be reliably used in practical concerns of when to live and when to die. Never a simple matter, today science and technology, laws and courts, politics and social policy, have made it impossibly abstruse and complex. We must look somewhere else to find our way.

FOURTEEN

A Matter of Personal
Responsibility

But that the dread of something after death,
The undiscover'd country, from whose bourn
No traveller returns, puzzles the will,
And makes us rather bear those ills we have
Than fly to others that we know not of?

SHAKESPEARE, *Hamlet*

Percy Williams Bridgman was an American physicist who pioneered high-pressure techniques, and who won a Nobel prize in 1946 as a result. He was eighty years old in 1961. He was incurably and painfully ill of Paget's disease, a progressive and disabling disease of the bones, and (being a scientist), he judged, quite coolly, that August 20 would be the last day on which he would remain strong enough to take the necessary action. On that day he shot himself to death, after writing a note condemning society for forcing him to do this alone, and without help or sympathy.

THESE WORDS were written by science fiction writer Isaac Asimov in tribute to a great scientist. Was Professor Bridgman justified in ending his life when and in the manner that he did? Was his act one of courage or cowardice, or was it, as he believed, purely the result of reason and logic? And what of his condemnation of society for forcing him to be and act alone? And who am I to judge?

Although my knowledge of Bridgman's life and how he died is limited to what Asimov wrote, it does seem safe to say that he did not die gracefully. Not that we can say the choice or means was wrong, but he died with bitter condemnation in his mind.

His complaint was that he did not have support from people who knew how he felt, "forcing" him to be alone at his time of greatest need. Had support been available, would his decision to die have been the same? Or would caring people have given additional meaning to his life, so he might have preferred to stay alive? Whatever his decision would have been, without the basis for his bitterness, he might have lived or died with grace.

We can only speculate about the reasons he felt alone and without help. However, I know from my own experience how difficult it is for those who care about me to be there and nurture when they are offended by what I want, or cannot tolerate the unpleasant feelings I have. I know it is hard for me to hear the pain of those I love. And who, indeed, can abide such pain, if a loved one wants to die? So the "cry for help" often goes unheard. Then the original despair is further compounded by feeling misunderstood and isolated.

If I hear a friend cry for help, I must not stand idly by and accept what is happening. I must try to rescue the person, if I can see another way. But the most important thing of all is that I continue to stand by with an outstretched hand, regardless of whether he wants to live or to die. Then he does not have to go or stay alone.

If he sees respect in my eyes, no matter what he feels or wants to do, he is more likely to act with responsibility and grace. Knowing he is not alone may change his mind, because his thoughts and acts will now include me, as well as him. And even if he does not change his mind, he is not alone, and he can go wherever he may choose, with confidence and dignity, free of anger or regret. Without that precious gift, he would truly be alone, and would have to live or die in the opposite of grace, what we might call "dis-grace."

Professor Bridgman's condemnation indicts all who have denied a friend support because he held a different view. And that need not be the case, for it is the person that needs support and not his view. When we do offer our support in time of need, we ennoble everyone, and that is of greater magnitude than any individual choice to live or die.

A woman I know has followed a very different route from Bridgman's. In her early sixties she suffered a minor stroke that left her only slightly incapacitated. Before that she had been physically very active, usually doing things for others. When her husband died, her daughter, with whom she had always had a close relationship, welcomed her into her home.

Then she suffered another stroke that left her partly paralyzed, with difficulty speaking. Her increased incapacity required more and more of her daughter and son-in-law's time and help. Their two formerly well-adjusted children began to suffer, with grades dropping precipitously, and the elder was arrested on a drug charge.

There was increasing tension between her daughter and her son-in-law, which culminated in a temporary separation. The poor woman could see that her presence was adding stress to those she loved most, yet she felt helpless to do anything about it. She confided in her one good friend that she wanted to die—she said she had lived a good and useful life before, but now was a useless burden to herself and those who cared about her.

Finally she and her daughter agreed that she should go to a nursing home. She was relieved that she no longer was interfering in her family's lives, but disliked it there. And in the absence of the thoughtful care she had received from her daughter, her physical problems grew rapidly worse. When she could no longer dress herself, she was either left in bed or forced to sit up all day in one position in a wheelchair (tied in, so she would not fall out).

In a few months she became incontinent, so she was kept in bed and had to begin wearing diapers. After that the only times she spoke were when she was visited by family and her friend. However, she confided only to her friend —not mentioning any subject to her daughter that she thought might upset her. To her friend she complained how humiliating it was to wear diapers. Again and again she told of her wish to die.

When alone, she began to moan pitifully. So she was sedated "to make her more comfortable" (often it is more for the benefit of staff and the other patients). The last report was that she lay in bed in a fetal position, wearing diapers, often groaning, and usually staring straight ahead or with eyes closed.

She continues to recognize family members when they

visit, although she has very little to say to them, or they to her. When her friend visits, she does talk, saying over and over that she wants to die, and asking, "Why does God not take me away from this?"

It has now been five years since she began to wish for death. In that time her body has been kept alive, but her spirit has withered. She says she is a useless burden to herself and to those who care about her. To those who "manage" her in the nursing home, she is, largely, an economic commodity. She has become a nearly anonymous member of the "living dead."

She certainly is not enjoying life. She lives—no, she exists—in pain, humiliation, and emptiness, feeling guilty and ashamed for how her continued existence affects her family. Fortunately, she has one friend in whom she can confide her only wish—that she should die. However, she does not die, and is helpless to take any action.

And neither has she asked for help to die. Perhaps she does not know it as an option, or, if she does, has chosen "no." Often she does not eat at all for a time; then she is fed by tube. We cannot say what is in her mind, except that she does not want to live, and that she does not live in grace. We can only wonder at what her response might be if someone were to offer to help her die.

Both she and Dr. Bridgman had to suffer in isolation, and come to terms with life or death all alone. Can anyone truly know his mind without awareness of the wider options that exist, or without supportive people to help in thoughtfully considering them?

A Matter of Personal Responsibility · 165

We live in an age when the self and the individual are the most important boundaries, yet our rituals continue as they did when the individual was less important than the crown, the master, the land, and the family. This leaves the individual with new personal freedoms, but without the support of communal rituals for his personal decisions. If we really believe in personal freedom of choice, we must find ways of instituting it with social supports.

Disease and age do not necessarily deprive a person of involvement with life, but they usually will eventually, if one lives long enough. The capacities that people prized most in themselves no longer remain. Most people lose their independence and, without an extended family, are separated from whom and what they love.

They are maintained in retirement homes, nursing homes, and convalescent hospitals. Although the quality of these facilities may vary from posh to spare, and the care from kind to callous, the residents are not with their family or friends. Sometimes they trudge along on joyless outings, like tired herds. They are surviving, and they are superfluous.

Some are kept artificially alive in institutions—more accurately, they are maintained there as if they were alive. For they live biologically, but in worlds of dimmed awareness and atrophied feelings and thought, reduced to the most primitive level. This is one of many examples that proves that if a technology is available, it is likely to be both used and abused.

In Orwell's *1984,* the place where executions took place

is named "The Ministry of Love." With the same cruel irony, the later years of life are called the "golden years." I fully understand and fully support all efforts to remove the elderly and the disabled from harmful and demeaning stereotypes and reduced opportunities. But that should also include the euphemistic stereotypes that block facing problems realistically. The elderly who wish to live deserve every support to do so—but with dignity. Unfortunately, very few have that support, and instead live under conditions in which they feel degraded, lonely, and hopeless. Many say clearly that they would prefer to be dead.

The human warehouse is an appalling sight, and it must be remembered that this is *not* God's creation, but man's. God's creatures naturally follow the life cycle of birth, growth, maturity, reproduction, and death. We now interfere with the last of these, and as a result, masses of elderly are kept from God's surcease in man-made limbo.

We make it hard to die for many different reasons. Besides the medical, there are the historical, legal, political, and religious reasons already discussed. There are also deeply personal ones. We want to feel we have done "everything humanly possible" for those we love and care about. To do less would be to feel guilty.

Fortunately, many such decisions are made well before they reach a conscious level; the spirit and the body give out together. Only when they do not, or when lifesaving medical technology keeps someone alive without his willing participation, does death become an issue.

Since what happens to a person's mind and spirit after

death is uncertain, and since we fear the unknown, we also are afraid of death. We certainly do not wish to place our loved ones and ourselves in jeopardy. So we "play it safe," and in spite of all the pain and suffering felt, impoverished lives are prolonged automatically.

The sad fact is that although our society is willing to provide the resources to keep people alive, very often it is without means to insure opportunity or dignity—conditions that for some make death preferable.

It is all well and good for us to declare what should be in the future, but it is of no benefit to those who must live with a demeaning reality in the present. The young who suffer can look to a better future with hope, but the old have only now. So we must consider seriously what they want now.

Even the most preliminary consideration of honoring someone's wish to die causes me to personally recoil. To support people in ending their lives is the antithesis of my life's commitment to save lives. Yet I would consider death as an option for myself, and I would need the help of someone else if I chose to die rather than live in degradation.

Should I not be willing to do for others what I would want for myself? Compassion requires me to give it serious consideration. My recoiling at the prospect, and the reluctance of others to consider it, may largely be a matter of self-interest and lack of courage—fearing that we might be held responsible for what we dare not judge.

Of course there are other very good reasons for reluctance: the fear that someone who did not want it, or someone who might recover, was put to death. Making a mistake in matters of life and death is a horrific responsibility; it is the one mistake that cannot be repaired.

Depression is a great deceiver, and it keeps people from making rational decisions about life and death. When depression lifts, what appeared to be hopeless may seem to be only a very small problem. Moreover, when depressed, a person is unlikely to realize it. That should be sufficient reason for anyone contemplating taking his life to doubt his judgment.

We seem, as a society, to have less reluctance about placing people in a living purgatory of suffering without hope than we do about helping them have a graceful death. Once born, a person is precluded from exercising his right to die. Society insists that he must continue to live however miserable his circumstances. Since it is man's will, not God's, that we are confronting, why should the person concerned not have freedom of choice?

If one has the audacity to become a physician, life-and-death decisions are made each day. Although most medical decisions are not clear-cut and have considerable margin for error, both doctors and patients think making the decision is worth the risk. So is it not also worth the risk when we consider a patient's desire to die?

If there should be a time to die, when is it, and how are we to know when it has arrived? By what criteria can we judge the value of life? How do we know when the situation is hopeless? How are we to judge when we are sustaining life without meaning? How do we know a life without purpose from one with it?

We cannot! There are innumerable different views, so it cannot be a judgment that any designated "we" can make. Whether a person's life is meaningful is subjective, and the most deeply personal of decisions. No one except I can say whether my life has meaning. Other people may be able to speculate how it might be for them under similar circumstances, or think my life *should* have meaning to me, but only I can know what is in my heart.

The moment we take that judgment from the individual is the same moment humanity is lost and the eras of Big Brother and Brave New World have begun. To wrest this most deeply personal choice from the individual, to place it in the hands of another, whether benevolent or malicious, is ethical rape.

When Patrick Henry made his famous declaration "Give me liberty, or give me death!" he was referring to his civil liberties. However, the same phrase could well apply to the choice between living in pain and discomfort, without purpose and gaining surcease through death. The freedom to choose is life's most vital decision. Should anyone be allowed to take that decision away from the person himself? I think not.

No one who wishes to live, and can do so without endangering others, no matter what personal difficulties he faces, should *ever* have that right taken from him. But by the same token, if someone has nothing but suffering in the future, without the possibility of recovery, should the person be punished for wishing to bring his suffering to the only end that is possible?

If a decision has been made, support should also be available for its implementation. A person should not have to be alone at this critical juncture—that by itself would certainly bias his decision. This is the time when a person most needs the support of loved ones or, where they are not available, other caring, concerned, and competent people.

In matters of life and death we must be especially wary of anything proposed as a "social good." Although we always seek a better social order, vigilance is necessary lest it become a tyranny by the strong or by the majority over individual rights. From Torquemada's Inquisition to Hitler's Third Reich to Pol Pot's killing fields, innocent victims serve to warn us of the dangers.

The awesome choice to live or die belongs not to the courts, to attorneys, to hospitals, to doctors, to nurses, or to any other group, but to the person whose life it is. The support of others is vital for an informed decision, so family, friends, and professionals can be of help, insofar as they can assist the individual's free choice.

That is the essence of being alive—being able to choose; otherwise we live only by instinct, like insects, or by the orders of others, like robots. And the most important choice one ever has is between life and death.

For me the principle seems clear, but the interpretation is the puzzle. When I can no longer spend a little time each day in something that is of value to someone else or me, and there is no reason to believe change is possible, then I am already dead in spirit. To end my biological life would be a mere formality.

However, I have found, to my surprise and sometimes consternation, that what I thought would prove unbearable turned out not to be. The reality was always different than I anticipated. It contained possibilities that were beyond me, until I was there.

Before I became paralyzed, I thought not being able to walk or run would be unbearable, and I would want to die. Indeed I did, but then, although my paralysis did not change, the opportunities seemed to grow.

During the last fifteen years I have seen my already sharply limited abilities fade, one by one. Each was a discouraging landmark, full of ominous portent, whether small or large, for each had also been hard gained. I could no longer spoon soup, could not sit up to eat, could not sit at all in anything but my own wheelchair, could not breathe when sitting up, had to return to using the iron lung, could no longer fly by plane, then no longer ride in a car, and on and on.

Most were permanent changes, a few were not. But something different usually emerged with each, something more than expected. So what I thought would be the right time for my escape from life, was not yet.

I know that I do not want to live only because I am afraid to die, or because others are afraid to let me die. And I want to allow others the same standards I would take for myself; it seems only fair.

Life is a gift, and I appreciate its preciousness. It deserves to be treated with the utmost respect, and wisely as well. However, with a true gift, the recipient is free to choose what to do with it.

I have been doubly blessed by being given a second opportunity for life after a life-threatening illness. During the years of hospitalization and disability, I have often felt useless and without purpose.

I learned what a living death can be. And I do not believe that being technically kept alive in serious discomfort without meaning or purpose is anything less than a violation of the sanctity of life.

There is a time to die, and there is probably a time when a person waits too long. How many families have been destroyed by maintaining a terminally ill member in a prolonged state of misery? How many people have been depleted of love by pain and physical suffering? How many people have lost their physical resources—home, job, and savings—because of the medical tragedy of a loved one?

I would willingly trust in God to decide the right time for me to die, but I dare not entrust that to a stranger, and certainly not to a hospital or legal committee. Someday it will become meaningless for me to continue the struggle. It will be the right time for me to die. I can only hope that I will know and that I will handle my life with grace.

There are no reliable or entirely objective criteria for knowing the right time to die, and to some extent they would be irrelevant anyway. For example, Lael T.

Wertenbaker in *Death of a Man* describes how her husband, suffering from cancer, struggled with the decision to live or die, but eventually hung on until the last possible moment before ending his life. At the other extreme was the much-publicized case of a woman with cancer who, soon after she knew, bid goodbye to friends and family and took her life. Even though an autopsy revealed that her cancer was in an early stage and she could have lived much longer, she had lived and died on her own terms.

Timing *is* a subjective matter, and it usually *is* the "right time" when we are being true to our hearts and convictions. To do the very best we can and to make the best choices that we can should be quite enough for all of us, because to be human is to be fallible. When we aspire to the perfections of a God, knowing full well that we will all fall short, we can realize the full nobility of man.

I have made what preparations I can. My living will explicitly forbids life supports of any kind beyond those I already use. I have given my wife, who knows my wishes, my durable power of attorney. I hope I can arrange it so that no one else will play any part in my deliverance. I would like no one else to have to bear any responsibility for what is my choice and mine alone.

I do not engage in most traditional religious rituals, but there are times when I know I am in synchrony with whatever forces there are in the universe. The choices that come from me then are right, even when they surprise me, and they sometimes do. They do not seem to be made alone; if that guiding force is God, it is in him or her that I trust.

But although the universe may point the way, my experience has been that it's up to me to get there. Since there is so little that I can physically do for myself, I must have plans and help to carry them out. Otherwise I may go past the right time.

FIFTEEN

To Celebrate a Choice

If I am not for me, who will be?
If I am only for me, what am I?
If not now, when?

HILLEL

THERE IS much reluctance about taking responsibility for one's life, and even more about taking responsibility for one's death—and understandably so. Important historical, religious, social, psychological, and legal reasons make suicide a taboo subject, one that is associated with much shame and guilt.

In the bygone era when monarchies flourished, people's lives did not belong to them, but to their king. If someone committed suicide, he was committing a crime against the king by depriving him of a servant. Even contemporary laws against suicide have historical roots traceable to this. Although the era of kings is gone, the choice to end one's life is still not a private act, but remains in the public domain. Even though people in the United States strongly believe that they are free to choose in other areas of their lives, laws against suicide continue in many places.

The opposition of religions has a very different origin, and is based on interpretations of morality. Life is sacred, and man should not interfere with it. The position is that since God is the creator of life, only He should have the right to end it. Suicide, then, is a crime against God.

However, as I described earlier, man has already interfered with nature in so many ways that it is no longer easy to tell God's will from man's. Besides, it is difficult to see God's will in the institutions where masses of elderly, many of whom would welcome death, are artificially kept alive. It is a sad and lonely spectacle that cries out for an alternative.

Death is an inevitable consequence of life. No one ever survives it. The old adage that nothing is certain except death and taxes is correct only about death. It is, at least for the body, permanent, so it cannot be undone.

We have no firsthand knowledge of the subjective experience of death, so each person and each group is free to project whatever beliefs they hold about it. Any criticism of any belief will have no more scientific credibility than the belief itself. One is as good as the next.

The hard-nosed insist there is no afterlife, only nothing. According to this view, no reward or punishment exists, and whatever life occurs on earth is all there is. Our only fate is to become inanimate matter for eternity.

One person will see only endless terror, while another sees a beautiful heaven. One group says that in death a person goes "to his reward"; another says his fate will be "eternal damnation." Hindus envision a succession of reincarnations in different forms, ending in purification. Among Christian and Moslem sects there are a wide variety of specific ideas to choose from. Many believe that earthly experience is but a preparation for an afterlife, and a judgment will be made in the hereafter that will determine punishment or reward for one's earthly endeavors.

We fear the unknown, so we try to fill it in some way —with hopes and beliefs to cover the fear. At other times we ignore or deny death's possibility so we will not be immobilized with fear—people often do that each time they fly in a plane or drive on the freeway. The unknown can be intolerable. So we challenge death, and laugh at it. And sometimes we even try to face it bravely, to overcome it—deliberately plunging into it, to get it over with.

With so many reservations about death, it is surprising that people take their own lives so frequently. Tragically, most who do have psychiatric problems from which they could recover if only appropriate treatment were available.

Suicide is the seventh most frequent cause of death among all people in the United States, and the leading cause among teenagers. It is sad to think that of these adults and teenagers, nearly all could have lived long and useful lives once they emerged from their depressive crises. The momentary assessments of hopelessness they make are unrealistically skewed by their depressed outlook.

The wrong people seem to be dying. Not only is there an epidemic of youth suicide, but increasing numbers of children are dying from drug problems and gang violence in the cities. Infant mortality in the United States is at a scandalously high level, considering how much is spent on health care. The children of grape pickers are dying from pesticides, and more and more children of both rural and urban parents are being born with birth defects. Even the AIDS plague affects more of the young than old.

Nature will ultimately have its way. When life gets out of balance, compensatory mechanisms develop to set things right. "Thinning of the herd" in the wild occurs naturally when demand outstrips supply. We seem to be in the beginning of such a process for the human herd, but it seems to have gone awry.

Many of what is potentially the hardiest group—the young—are being thinned while the old and weak are being kept alive. Even some of our politicians now dare to express concern that there may soon be too many unproductive elderly, supported by too few people of working age.

We expect that the old will die; they are supposed to. As part of the ever-renewing life cycle, they die to make room for the young. But the irony is that they are now being kept alive in the unhappiest of circumstances, while the young, who should be alive, seem to be dying for them.

Many of the old no longer fear death, but welcome it as surcease from their infirmities, their pain, and their lack of purpose. They fear a "life sentence."

They fear going to an institution; they fear being separated from what and whom they love; they fear losing who and what is familiar; they fear having little or no control over their lives; they fear being vulnerable and taken advantage of; they fear being poor and lonely. They fear survival without hope for the future—life without meaning. They welcome death.

I began my medical career before antibiotics were widely available. I often heard doctors at that time refer to pneumonia as "the old man's friend." It was a quiet and merciful way for the elderly's lives to end, sometimes at home, or sometimes during a brief hospitalization.

When antibiotics became readily available, almost no one died of uncomplicated pneumonia any more. We were elated, and saw only good coming from these miracles. But when I now visit an institution for the old and infirm, I feel like the sorcerer's apprentice, who played with magic he did not fully understand. When I see their unhappy empty silence, and when I hear their groans and cries, I hear their indictment of our hubris. When I hear them say they want to die, I think there must be a better way.

Antibiotics and other medical progress have been a great boon to mankind, but we did not anticipate the new problems we created with them, problems for which we as yet have no solution.

There are no easy, and perhaps not even any acceptable, political or social responses to this imbalance. However, there may be individual and personal solutions, which could in turn positively affect society. That is, if it were possible and acceptable for the elderly in poor health to have a larger part in determining how long they would live, there might be some restoration of balance.

Not long ago I spent several hours with two friends of over thirty years. Both are physicians, each with a well-justified reputation for outstanding achievement in his specialty. Much of the time was spent catching up with one another's lives.

We are all now senior citizens, and even they are beginning to show signs of aging. We began to talk of living and dying, something each of us has known about from work but that has stronger personal meaning as we grow older. My two friends must face death with their patients on a daily basis, since one spends much of his time with cancer work, and the other with AIDS.

The cancer specialist said that if he got cancer, unless it were very localized and almost certainly completely curable, he would not accept radiation or chemotherapy. His main goal would be pain control and his comfort, and he would want to take as much medication as necessary to achieve that goal. He added that at a certain point, the dosages would be so high that it would be incompatible with life. I interpret that to be "doctor talk" for taking his life.

The friend who works with AIDS patients frankly said that he thought he would end his life if he got the disease. These two men are well adjusted and competent, with outstanding reputations and with loving families. They each had a strong religious upbringing, although in different faiths, and have strong moral values. They have thought about the meanings of life, and lived in exemplary ways.

They, as much as anyone, know about the experiences of suffering, pain, and disability, and how they can erode the human mind and spirit. Although each now enjoys life, each also plans to take whatever steps are necessary to avoid prolonged suffering and meaningless life. Indeed, useless heroics for the elderly may be no more than a form of approved sadomasochism.

Physicians know from experience the difference between a "good death" and a hard one. They see little or no advantage in meaningless suffering, and they know how it can reduce the person to a humiliated subhuman level. My friends have the knowledge and means to prevent such degradation from overtaking them, and they would do everything possible to keep it from happening to them. They are luckier than most people, for they can keep some control of their lives.

However, their patients are prevented by well-meaning legal and social strictures, and the power of public opinion, from considering all of the options available to them. We must somehow remove the question of choosing to live or die from the arena of conflicting ideologies bent on making each case into a public policy discussion. The individual's choice in the matter becomes obscured by these abstract discussions, as though a general principle were to be maintained. We must discover ways to place the decision back into the hands of the person whose life is at stake.

For most of us it is hard to find enough support in ourselves alone, and we need it in whatever decision we must make. People should not be made to feel guilty for their choices if no harm to others is done. We offer such support in other less critical and controversial "rites of passage" such as marriage, coming of age, graduation, birth, and christening. Why should people be deprived of experiencing in life the love and affection expressed at their funerals?

A rite of passage for one in need and near the end of life could perhaps be used to buttress a free choice to live or die. It might require a series of such rites to assure the person's free choice. The tradition of a funeral, as useful as it may be to those who survive a death, does nothing for the one who is gone. Should we not provide as much support to those considering such an awesome choice, as we do to celebrate them after they are gone?

We have models for this rite of passage in the ends of Jesus' and Socrates' lives on earth. Before the day they died both were surrounded by the people they cared for most—Jesus at the Last Supper, and Socrates in his jail cell. There vital choices were made. The difference was that Socrates had support, while Jesus was denied it. Both died with grace: Jesus despite betrayal, and Socrates with the aid of kind concerned support.

That Jesus was graceful in his death, when it had occurred under such trying circumstances, made it a magnificent triumph of the spirit. But try as we may, few if any of us have such divine qualities, and so at the very least, in part, must depend on earthly supports. Whether God is alive or dead or never was, we all must rely on others, and are especially in need of concerned human contact when we, mortals, are facing the awesome choice between life and death.

A rite of passage such as this would also benefit the loved ones left behind, for goodbyes left unsaid may continue to torment the living. The loved ones may not agree with the actions planned and may see them as a terrible mistake, so the proper farewell may or may not cause a change of mind. Whatever decisions are finally reached, loved ones' views must be given equitable weight and require thoughtful, loving negotiation, for we do not walk alone.

Even in the face of death, a person still has responsibilities to the lives that will continue. Since memories will remain alive, the needs of those who love and care must be thoughtfully attended to. To be surrounded by loved ones at such a critical time of choice would solidify the link between those who live now and those who have gone before—the sacred connection that binds us to eternity.

But I can hear the voices of protest saying how macabre such a rite would be. But is it really a mad or futile dream to hope for a celebration of human choice? To hope that all the friends and family would gather around to support the person? Would it not be better than the way it is— with the person concealing such thoughts, or acting alone, in secrecy, without support?

Since the elderly or chronically ill must rely heavily on others for their care, safeguards should assure the individual that the choices made were his or hers alone, and that it was the integrated he or she who made it. The assurances should be these at least:

First, that the choice made is not primarily to serve the

advantage of others. The person considering life or death is usually physically and mentally dependent on others, so he should be protected against their trying to force their own material or spiritual beliefs on him, whether with benign or nefarious intent. This must not be construed to suggest that others cannot express and teach their views; however, necessary physical and mental support should not be contingent on compliance with them.

Second, that the condition that made living too much to bear was permanent, and a near-miracle would be necessary for any substantial improvement to occur. People who can be expected to recover from an illness need consistent support, through information and reassurance, to confirm that this is true. Without such knowledge, even the temporary misery of something like the flu might make life unbearable.

Depression is a special case. It applies to all illness generally because poor health nearly always creates some degree of depression and despair, while at the same time depression can be profound when there is no apparent reason. Its essence is a loss of hope that seems to preclude improvement. The future is bleak because there seems no chance of anything better. Suicide without depression is quite rare.

Both depression and suicide increase in old age, as they could be expected to, because the future—at least on earth —grows shorter by the day. As the chances of another day are less, so too are those for a better day. So the old and infirm know they may never see a better day.

Those who believe in an afterlife have a substantial

edge. For them the future may not be so bleak at any age, for it is yet to come. They will not despair while on this earth, for they do not see an end. Whether they are right or not is not the subject here. My concern is how they feel in life and, even more, how they act in it. All of us should act in reverence for what is here now: people, their thoughts and feelings, other creatures, the plants and trees, the earth itself.

Freedom to choose is an essential quality of human life which is widely accepted in most countries. Thus, to offer informed yet respectful support—not contingent on shared beliefs—for an individual's freedom to choose between life or death is reverence for that life. All life is perishable, and extending its "shelf life" beyond its essence does not benefit us or whoever created us.

There would be other advantages as well to letting people make their individual choices. Those who live in what are now overburdened facilities for the aged would have freely elected to be there. Those who choose not to continue to live would have found their peace painlessly, with dignity and support.

SIXTEEN

A Graceful Way to Die

No wind favors him who has no destined port.

MONTAIGNE, *Essays*

ONCE WHEN I WAS six or seven, my father gave me a dime to buy an ice cream cone, a double-decker at a nickel a scoop. I walked half a block from our family bicycle store to the corner where the Givens and Cannon Drug Store was located, stepped up to the soda fountain counter, and asked for one scoop of chocolate and one of strawberry.

The waitress, who recognized me, winked and dug out two extra-heaping scoops of Knudsen's best. She neatly wrapped a napkin around the base of the cone and handed it to me as I put my dime on the counter for her to take. Then, as I assessed the overloaded cone, trying to decide where I should lick first, disaster struck! The top scoop fell on the floor. I stared dumbstruck at the floor, and then back at the partly empty cone. It seemed like tragedy of this magnitude had never happened to me before.

Charlie Givens watched from behind the prescription counter and, on seeing my dismay, stepped out and put his hand on my shoulder. Turning to the already sympathetic waitress, he magnanimously said, "Give the boy another scoop." She did, and with a smile. I mumbled thanks, and to cover my embarrassment hurried out onto the sidewalk.

However, I remained so unnerved that as I walked back toward the family store, I hardly tasted my favorite flavors. What continued to puzzle me was this: I had received the ice cream cone I had paid for, and it was in my possession when it fell. Givens and Cannon Drug Store owed me nothing more; the responsibility was mine. Given that, why was I rewarded with another chance, a complete cone? Simple justice dictated that since it was my fault, I did not deserve a replacement scoop.

I was very grateful for their kindness, but I was also confused by it. If good things could happen without apparent reason, then so could bad ones, too. Where was the justice in that? And since I was taught that justice was one of our highest ideals, something that people should strive for in their relationships with one another, I fervently believed in it.

But nature is not ruled by men's beliefs in justice; it operates by its own laws. I have grudgingly learned, kicking and screaming all the way, that life is not always just and fair. The "race" is not even always "to the swift" either. More often than not, the events in life fail to reward much that is good, and fail to punish much that is bad. Hard work does not necessarily result in success, nor indolence in failure.

Does that mean we should abandon all faith in justice? Not at all, for events are not simply random. Knowing what you are striving for does seem to help a lot, and planning and effort will help even more. The chances of reaching what one wants *do* grow with planning, work, skill in implementation—and, of course, support from others.

But simply setting your course and following through is not enough. Call it fate, call it destiny, call it God's will, call it what *you* will, there is something out there in the stars or beyond that also determines how the hand is played.

I did not deserve to be given life—that certainly was a gift. But I did not deserve to become paralyzed, either. I did not deserve to find a new way to live with it, but I did. Neither will I deserve to die when that time comes. No one deserves much of anything, as far as I can see. But we are better off if we can treat whatever we get as fortune's gift to us.

Although I may not be the captain of my ship, I am the steward. And as the steward, I must see to the details of the voyage and the comfort and well-being of all of those on board. I am responsible for the trip, but with very little authority for its destination and time of arrival. As steward, I want to do my job well, and to the end.

When I first became paralyzed, I wanted very much to die. Yet even then, "how" mattered to me. To simply slip away seemed not enough. I wanted to feel responsible and useful, if not in life, at least in death. Since I could see no way of being useful in my life as it was, I looked for some means of usefulness in my death.

How desperate I was to find one! I tried to think of any

way that an expenditure of my life could be of benefit to others.

One grandiose fantasy I had went like this: some cataclysmic event threatened the world, like World War II all over again—something in which to me one side seemed clearly aligned with good, the other committed to evil. A suicide mission was necessary to save the day for good. It was a solitary sacrificial mission, requiring nothing physical, but a single person of clear mind. Timing was more important than strength to do the job. Sometimes in the fantasy there was a single switch that had to be thrown, and it could be operated by the slightest movement of my head, the only part of me over which I had voluntary control.

As crazy as that now sounds, it was a clumsy beginning effort to come to terms with feeling useless in life, and with the uselessness of death. We are doomed from the beginning, but that is not all we are. We live by human metaphors in a world not created by men, but gods. So everything we say and think is paradox and irony.

Perhaps our greatest gift is when we have a glimpse into what it is like from above, when we see the irony of our lives in humor or in other moments of enlightenment. Then we stand in awe and reverence of the wonder of it all.

We are destined to live by the stories that we tell. If life is a game, eventually we all must lose. In the court of life, we are all sentenced to death. In the wars of life we will ultimately not be the conquerers, but the vanquished ones.

And in the stories of life, we will be the butt of jokes as as often as we are the hero.

However, life is much more than just a simple story we can write. We can author what it is we strive to find. Even if it seems like a game, we can still play it well and fair. If we see it as a court, we can do our best to make it just. The world is not a machine that we designed, but we can aspire to understand its works, and although we probably never will, we can try.

And so it is with death: we cannot know truly what it is until it is too late. Yet we can still plan for it as though we knew. There is no reason I can expect to have it just my way; still, the chances will be better if I make my own plans.

Here are stories of some people who I think died well and with grace.

The first person was a hard-driving, controlling businesswoman who had difficult relationships with everyone. She sought to dominate her business, her children, and her husband.

When she was in her late sixties, her heart began to fail. She rejected extensive surgery as an option, and set as her major task placing her affairs in order. In her case that was a tall order, since she had held things under tight rein. Despite pain, shortness of breath, and precious little energy, she settled her business affairs gradually with the same meticulous care that had developed them. The process took over two years.

She simultaneously spent as much time as possible with

her family, deliberately working to emancipate them from her control. Family members at last felt free to express their long-suppressed anger toward her, and she patiently accepted it, for the first time, without counterattack. She took it all, despite her failing energies. The process of healing these relationships was frequently interrupted by extended periods of hospitalization. Sometimes it seemed that only her will to complete what remained unfinished kept her going.

At last she told her family that her work was done, and soon she would die. She had never been so warm and uncharacteristically accepting. Once, only days before she died, the doctor grew alarmed by her decline, and insisted on diagnostic X rays. She dismissed the idea as wasteful, and with a laugh rhetorically asked, "What for?" The doctor was adamant and tried to explain their necessity, assuring her that she was not dying, that they would help, and finally that they were hospital policy. Very unlike her old self, she acquiesced, with a gently repudiating laugh: "If you must, you must." She had transcended her need to control.

The night she died, she received many visitors and had many warm exchanges. Then, growing weary, she told them she would die soon, and wanted to be alone. A few hours later she did die peacefully, in her sleep. By then she had completed her work on earth.

The next case is that of Paul Richards, the famous major league catcher and manager. Other than his baseball fame, all that I know of him is from an obituary on radio, delivered by the celebrated baseball announcer Red Barber, who at the time was in his eighties.

The part I remember was essentially this: that Paul Richards died a "good death," just as he had lived a good life. Richards was well along in years, long since retired. Although he also had a weak heart, golf was his passion, and he played daily. He died instantaneously on the golf course while swinging at the ball.

He died "with his boots on," doing what he loved to do. No pain, no major incapacity; it was just as he wished his death to be. It was not only a "good death," it was an easy one.

But a graceful death may not be easy if one must be a witness to his own deterioration, and watch in pain as the end draws too slowly near. Here are two examples of when death was not so easy, yet was faced with refinement and dignity.

The first concerns a recent death, the mother of a good friend. In her eighties, she fell and badly broke her hip and pelvis. During a painful, extended hospitalization, her memory deteriorated, and at times she had frightening hallucinations that she was being attacked.

Through it all she retained a friendly disposition, cheerfully smiling whenever anyone entered her room. What sustained her was a deep religious faith. She prayed whenever she was by herself, asking only that she be granted the strength to accept her fate.

Her memory failed so badly, that she was able to remember only two things: the faces, although not the names, of her immediate family, and God. Even in bouts of pain, she would mumble with a smile, "It's God's will."

She lingered on in nursing homes in considerable discomfort, often confused and sometimes irrational. Yet even when not comprehending, she tried to comfort others. She was never bitter, never angry at her fate, but accepted it to her last day, when life quietly left her. To the end she was well supported by her faith in God.

The final example was described by Norman Cousins in *Norm:*

The world of religion and philosophy was shocked recently when Henry P. Van Dusen and his wife ended their lives by their own hands. Dr. Van Dusen for more than a quarter of a century had been one of the luminous names in Protestant theology. He enjoyed world status as a spiritual leader. The news of the self-inflicted death of the Van Dusens therefore was profoundly disturbing to all who attach a moral stigma to suicide and regard it as a violation of God's laws.

Henry and Elizabeth Van Dusen had lived full lives. In recent years they had become increasingly ill, requiring almost continual medical care. They realized their infirmities were worsening, that they would soon become completely dependent on others for even the most elementary needs and functions. Under these circumstances, little dignity was left in life. They didn't like the idea of taking up space in a world with too many mouths and too little food. They believed they had the right to die when their time had come. It was precisely because they had placed the highest value on life that they didn't want life to become a caricature.

Yet the Van Dusens were deeply religious. They were not mentally disturbed. They saw no religious justification in the prolongation of life beyond meaning. They believed that those with nothing more to give to life, or to receive from it, should not be condemned because they regarded death as a natural part of life—even if death were self induced.

Each of these people died gracefully, although under very different conditions. Each was sustained to the end by a belief in the purposes of life and death. Yet those beliefs differed remarkably from one another.

Some elderly people accept the indignities of their failed health and make no effort to affect the final outcome, waiting until death takes them. Others choose to end their lives when they can see that there is no meaning left in them. Norman Farberow compared the histories of two terminally ill groups. He found that in dying, each person behaved as in life: the "implementers," who had taken control over the circumstances of their lives, chose when and how to end them, too. Those who had more passively allowed most of life to happen to them also did in death. And is that not the way that it should be, so that all will be with firm conviction and continuity?

The first woman saw life as something that must be controlled and manipulated, making her a fearful tyrant to many. When she recognized that she would soon be dead, true to her concern, she lent all her effort to encouraging those who would succeed her to competently be in charge. She wanted them to have control, and she wanted to be confident that the world remained secure and in good hands.

Her lifestyle was questionable at best, but, in the end, she wanted to see that what she left was well managed by others. This continuity of purpose was not from religious or philosophical commitment; it was a reaction to feeling vulnerable. Still, it allowed her to accept death with charity and dignity.

Life's meaning for the baseball great was in sport. Without it, life would have been useless and futile. He was fortunate to die before his capacity for sport was gone, and while fully engaged in what he believed in and loved.

The woman of simple and abiding religious faith was sustained by her beliefs. Her trust in "God's will" was so complete that she could endure pain, confusion, and fearful hallucinations with equanimity and hope to the very end.

The case of the Van Dusens was different still. They too were deeply religious; however, they saw no purpose in prolonging life when they had no more to give to it.

If there is continuity of meaning from life to death, it may help to ease the end. This was true for Paul Richards and sports, and my friend's mother and religious faith. However, it also may require lots of thought and work to accommodate the beliefs and purposes that were supports in life to the different realities of death. The controlling businesswoman and the Van Dusens had such tasks; careful planning was necessary to make death consistent with their lives' beliefs and actions.

One of the most hopeful things about death—as it is

with each developmental stage—is that it provides another chance to be the way you want. All is not lost when death is near, for it is another time when you can do things right.

The daughter of the controlling businesswoman had only regret and bitterness toward her mother until she neared the end. The mother whom she despised in life became a model of noble strength in death, one on which she could later draw in times of need. A considerate and upright death can begin to make amends for a wasted, thoughtless life. You cannot erase the past, but you can begin a new and finer purpose at the end.

When my time has come, first I hope that I will know it. That has been a mystery and quandary for me, as you have read here. Yet this is where I place my faith in the powers of the universe, with some good reason. For, although at other times of change I have often initially misread the direction signals, eventually they became quite clear.

Many times I thought the time had come—should have come—and I earnestly wanted it to be so. Yet as I paused to be certain that the signs I read were true, they changed. Life within me grew again, even though my body remained much the same. I knew that this was not the time. So with patience, and I hope a little forbearance too, I trust that I will know.

I would like my passage to be a celebration, surrounded by those I love. We would mainly just sit together, with perhaps a toast or two. We would also reminisce from time to time, and laugh a lot, and cry. If the party goes very well, we will not be able to tell the laughter from the tears. And when the party is finally over, we will say our goodbyes and the guests will leave, one by one. When the last one is gone, I will close my eyes, and quietly slip away.

To die with grace requires that one feel that what happens has been his choice. Yet the realities of life rarely conform to plans. So I need a good contingency plan as well—to meet the real, yet unexpected, design, known only to the one who makes it. It is a plan in which I must try to accept whatever comes *as if* it were of my design, even when it is not. To willingly accept what happens, with the same good repose as when the choice was mine, is what is meant by the phrase "Let thy will be mine."

SEVENTEEN

Gaia and We Are One

Death may not be funny, but it's not the end
of the world.

BUD BLITZER

BUD BLITZER is a friend, and an old quadriplegic polio like me. When he read this manuscript, he complained that it was not very funny—and then added the statement above. I assume he meant that there should be more important things to a person than his own death. If so, he joins the legions of others who have realized that recognizing meaning in your life, more than focusing merely on your own survival, makes living more fulfilling and death tolerable.

In the Age of Narcissism, people believe that the only meaning is in personal pleasure. They believe they are all alone, disconnected from family, friends, community, and state. They have to take care of "number one," since no one else will. Holding that belief creates a self-fulfilling prophecy, so they live in retreat from continuity and connection. They divorce frequently, do not live with parents or other relatives, move freely from one relationship to the next, shuttle their children from one parent to the next. They hardly know their next-door neighbors, do not participate in community affairs, and rarely know the names of their representatives in state and local government. They see little value in voting, believing it makes no difference. They live as if they are all alone.

I often felt entirely alone when I was first sick and in the hospital. People were there taking care of my basic needs, but not as I would have taken care of them. They usually had unfamiliar ways, and were neither family nor long-time friends. They were strangers, in spite of the fact that they dealt with my most private and life-sustaining functions.

I was separated from my own vital functions too, and they were managed mechanically by strangers. All of that made me feel estranged from myself, as well as from others. I longed to feel at one again. But that seemed impossible, since I no longer controlled the intimate details of my life.

Then miraculously I met my wife, who had an incredible ability to respond to my needs, much as I would have done myself. She made it possible for me to live almost as if I were not paralyzed at all. I felt restored to grace.

We grew older together, and I needed even more help at the same time that her own strength and skills began to slow. Then there was a more rapid decline in her strength —she developed a disabling rheumatoid arthritis, making most of my care nearly impossible for her. Once again I felt all alone.

We needed a small army of others to help us get along. I did have care that was more than adequate, but because it was done by others, of different needs and abilities, I was not at one with myself or others. Rita, my wife, had given me a reprieve from the separation that I felt between my needs and their fulfillment, and now that was changed again.

What made me feel alone was that when it concerned my person and the functions of my body, I expected people to be like me, and act as I would. My needs were being met, but not my way. I wondered, is it ever possible *not* to have such expectations, when it concerns what for everyone is private and intimate?

Of course I always knew and understood that everyone is unique, and everyone does things in different ways. But I had to find ways of accepting that reality when it dealt with the most intimate details of my life—like being fed, or using the bathroom. This could not be just a "good idea," for it was as personal as it could possibly be.

It is tempting to assume that is the way it is in life, that we really are separate and alone. And that all the meaning we can find is only a vain attempt to avoid facing the reality of our isolation. From this point of view the process of growing up is to accept despair.

It seemed to me that my only hope would be if I could find some larger and more essential purpose to which I could subordinate my personal needs for physical care— that is what I had already been able to do through work, my marriage, and my friends. But this now had to be something more, for I could see that as my health and strength declined I would have less time and energy to give to these purposes and so, less that I could receive from them.

Faith, it is said, is the antidote to fear, but for me to accept it, I would need evidence I could comprehend. I strongly mistrust "blind faith" alone, for the world has had too many fraudulent evangelists who have misused it to justify almost anything—including abuse, cruelty, their greed, and even the murder of those who would not agree.

When I first became paralyzed, I was more generally trusting and I had great faith in doctors, nurses, and hospitals. But I learned the hard way that to trust others completely was a dangerous thing. I have been dropped, burned, overdosed, permanently overstretched, given incorrect and dangerous pills, and on and on.

I cannot ignore the fact that these things occurred, and since I have been given a capacity to make prudent judgments, whatever the source, I can only presume that I am free to use that capacity, if no harm is done to others by using it. Still, sometimes it cannot help but further distance people.

I do not, please understand, doubt the good intentions of most of the people who did these things to me, and I am also grateful to them for the good things they did. But I have to draw upon my own experience and use my reason too. And what I learned was this: when you are completely helpless and in the hands of others, whatever good intentions they may have, it is wise to be on guard.

Those experiences have colored my faith in everything and made me cautious of where I place my trust. Although

I am not in charge of my life, and from experience know I cannot be, I still must try, because I am unsure of who *is* in charge or what their motives are. So, I often feel I am really all alone, and yet in need of the continuous help of others—not an easy thing.

So what grounds, if any, have I for faith—and in what? To begin with I know that I am here, and that is no small miracle. I can think and feel and sometimes act. I am aware —another miracle. And, like the universe itself, as men and women we are nothing if not creative. And if that is true, not to use that creativity to discover meaning here would be to give up a vital part of our capacity. Whether that meaning is that we are a temporary evolutionary develop- ment or God's creation in his own image does not change that our essence is creative, and our task is to use it wisely.

And that is where I do have faith and hope, that each situation encountered can be met creatively. When I have pain and illness I will do my best to alleviate it so I can be restored to health and rid of pain. And if I cannot, I am still not lost and can meet my suffering creatively by alter- ing the way I look at it.

I can consider what I can learn from this experience I did not choose or want. And there is always something. What is there in this pain, this loss, this particular adversity to teach me? I know that in each experience, good or bad, there is a further lesson that can serve me well.

And there is more, if all else fails. I can change the way I look at things: I can look past my fear to see with benign neutrality what I may have disdained before. And there is always something of awe and wonder, if I am looking through the window that affirms those things (see Chapter 6, "Looking for a Better View").

When I met Rita I no longer felt alone in a hostile universe, for she could respond to my needs as I would have if I had been able. Since any conflict between us was a threat, I would try to ignore it, and make believe that we were still in agreement. If that did not work for me, I would feel alone again.

Now that she is no longer able to care for me physically, and our lives are more separate, one might think I would feel alone again. Where we once did nearly everything together, we have developed separate interests, separate friends, and separate lives. Yet, I feel no loss of closeness, nor any less involved with her.

Gifts can come in many forms, if only I can allow myself to see beyond the very narrow limits that I create for myself. Opportunities will often not be seen, if I insist they must be only the ones I think that they should be. And kindness, too, has many different forms, that will not be seen unless I trust that in every loss there can also be a gain. There was a vital lesson here I would not have learned without this loss.

The loss I felt when Rita could no longer help me as she had, was also a gift disguised. I could see love more clearly now, could recognize that it was also there beyond the physical plane on which we had so cautiously built our lives. Rita and I are different in many ways—ones I now appreciate but dared not see before, for fear I would find myself alone. Loving gifts may come in separateness and differences, as well as in synchrony. And that vision could extend farther than the trusted few on whom I had come to rely.

Even though our lives have changed, there is more gain than loss. In development of comprehension, each of us follows a well-worn evolutionary path. The world is very small at first, revolving around our elemental needs and that which meets those needs. We slowly realize there is more and more out there—home and family, neighbors, schools and communities, then other lands and peoples, other planets, stars and galaxies. The boundaries of our worlds grow and grow, so why not begin to trust beyond what we now know, in what perhaps we will comprehend in time?

Those who help me now respond in many very different ways, but I find I can more often appreciate and enjoy those differences—even when it concerns my care, and that is something new. And they often bring awarenesses and skills beyond those that I could know myself. I do not at all give up my way, but I do give up that one is right, the other wrong.

When I am attached to my pains and meeting only my survival needs, I think of all my fears. But when I trust that in each loss there is a potential gain, and that it fits within a larger scheme, I am released and free. I still have far to go to know it all the time, but I know I am less attached to behaving as if I am the center of it all. My ability to see the ways in which I am not alone has grown and I can more clearly see that in so many ways, we are all a part of something larger.

I once considered the universal concept of God to be a mere illusion; it now seems to me that myself as center is just as much an illusion. Although both concepts are partly true, they exist on different planes and are seen through different windows. When what I see is guided only by my fears and criticism, I am limited to the struggle with my body; however, when I seek to find the wonder I know is there, I feel I enter a more elevated place.

Narrow-mindedness is what I must overcome, just as mankind must to achieve its destiny. Once kings were considered incarnate gods and their own peoples as the only ones of worth. And in each domain they believed it was the center of the whole universe. They knew the earth was flat, as any fool could plainly see, and that their land was at the center of all the stars and heavens. An organized and firmly believed system, but we now know it was wrong.

A few, like Copernicus and Galileo, could see with more open minds. They were disdained when they said the earth was neither flat nor the center of the universe. Today, we know the earth is round, and that no land or people can be the only center of it all. We no longer believe that kings can be divine and we know we are but a tiny part of something infinitely more complex and large. What the eye had seen, and the wise man said was true, were no more than illusions.

Tribal chauvinism supports such false beliefs. It has not disappeared, and is even on the rise in some places, and understandably so. For the universe is a place of such infinite size that every point within may be erroneously perceived as the center, so why not with every man. However, a broader understanding is evolving, one in which we all are seen as much alike, parts of some larger plan we cannot fully understand. I try to see creatively beyond my personal survival needs, so I can touch those larger meanings of it all.

We are all doing our evolutionary work, sometimes well, sometimes not so well, but in the service of something we cannot now fully comprehend. Whether it is those who help me in my care or anyone else, we are doing our work, playing our roles in an evolving cosmic process, each as important as the next, each of us experiencing ourselves at the center, while being challenged to see that there is more.

Nevertheless, it is not easy to stay creatively involved in a process beyond what we can comprehend intellectually. That is why most people concretize such thought in the form of a God whose wishes they believe they fully know. That is fine with me, if it does the job for them; in fact, it has advantages over insisting there is nothing at all. But by "knowing it all" they risk retreat to the same close-minded tribal chauvinism that made kings into gods and was certain that the earth was flat. Those who can trust their hearts completely may need nothing more, but I am still dependent on my intellect as well. So I look for ideas to support my heart.

A concept that appeals to me is the Gaia hypothesis. It

has been proposed by a maverick British scientist, James Lovelock, to account for serious gaps in Darwinian evolutionary theory. Living creatures normally change their environments until they become uninhabitable, first for other forms of life and then for themselves.

If evolution had performed only in accord with this, all life on earth would have died out by now, according to Lovelock. The processes of physics, chemistry, and biology would have automatically destroyed the very conditions that support life.

But life does continue, and he believes this would only be possible if everything on earth, even including the soil, the oceans, and the atmosphere, formed a single unified living organism. We would have had an inhospitable atmosphere, as on Mars and Venus, if it were not that some living process maintains the earth in homeostatic equilibrium, something that has continued since there was any life at all on earth.

Only some coherent organization of the whole earth could maintain just the right raw materials for life to continue. And the chemicals essential for life—oxygen, nitrogen, carbon dioxide, phosphorous, even the rarest essential elements—continue at constant, sustaining levels. And that would be possible only if there were some overall control system.

Like in a single person, where each living cell and organ plays a part in the homeostatic mechanisms that keep the body temperature livable and signal when food and water are needed, something within the earth must be able to sense changes, so that they can be exactly counteracted. Perhaps each of us is a cell or organ in that larger organization.

Lovelock called whatever is in control Gaia, the name the Greeks gave to the living goddess that was the earth (they also believed she could assume human form). She could be both harsh and loving, generous and stingy, like humans can be.

What Gaia represents for me is another name for the incomprehensible controlling system of which we are a part. I seem to need that kind of intellectual support to coincide with my faith in cosmic creativity. The American Indians held that larger view: that they all played equal parts, along with every living and inanimate thing, in serving the Great Spirit of the earth and universe. They were careful to take only what they needed to support themselves, apologizing to what they had to take for that necessity. They were reverent to both life and death.

Our individual and species survival may depend on finding new ways of showing reverence to all natural processes. No longer is it an intellectual and spiritual luxury to be concerned with the integrity of the earth—atom bombs, pollution, deforestation, greenhouse effects, make reverence for every creature and everything a necessity of growing urgency.

The universe will have its way, with or without mankind. But we have a chance, if we can align our will with those processes that are eternal. Our greatest challenge is to ourselves, to make our responsibilities to ourselves consistent with our responsibilities to each other, and to the earth and to the universe. "Thy will be done"—can we also make it ours?

And that is what I hope to do, to play my role the best way I can, and support others in playing theirs. When I encounter things I cannot change or control, and as I grow older there are more and more of them, I will still use my creativity, if I can, to see what I can learn. Even though it is often hard, I want to find the potential gain within each loss. I want to see the events of my life with the reverence they deserve, to see what they can affirm through the window of appreciation. That way I will be aligned with the creative forces of the universe, doing my small part.

Becoming totally paralyzed was a terrible narcissistic blow to me. Whatever sense of trust I had in myself and others was stripped away. Rita's responsive support to me slowly helped me get it back. I gradually could extend my trust in her to myself and to others, and then to realize it was all a part of something even more. I had to travel the developmental scale a second time.

People often say that if they had their lives to live over again, they would do it better by being able to take advantage of what they did not know the first time. Although I did not and probably would not have chosen it, I feel as if I have lived a second life.

In the first life things went my way, and as I planned them. Whatever I did seemed to work out much as I wanted it to. By the time it came to an end, and I got sick,

I had reached my goals. By age twenty-five I was a doctor, had won a national tennis championship, and had a rich social and love life.

The second life began with deficits that gradually became filled—with love and caring, first from my wife, then from others when I could accept their different ways. And I now can often see beyond the fulfillment of my immediate needs, and what I see is that I have only played my small part in the universal play.

Perhaps I did do it better the second time around.

EIGHTEEN

To Live and Die with Grace

This, too, shall pass.

I EXPECTED to live out my time on earth as strong and healthy. But it did not turn out that way.

The details of my life may seem so inconceivably different that some people may find it hard to think of me as being like them. They may see me as no more than the stereotype of a cripple. But even if the particulars of my life are unique, I am entirely ordinary and usual. For hardly anyone's life turns out as expected, and everyone encounters terrible losses, and has intolerable things done to him.

So I write about myself not because I think I am special, but more because I am so common, and what is in my life is in every life. The details may differ, but the issues remain the same. When I discover something about myself, I learn something about everyone. When I write about myself, it is my way of discovering the whole universe.

Each of us is special: the gift of individuality allows us a choice in how we live. Each of us is common, which provides us with a capacity to care for others as we do ourselves. This is the gift of compassion. These twin elements of being both separate and joined together create the paradox that makes us all humans.

As individuals, we can live on earth in time and space, as free men and women. We are also at one and joined together, which means we can touch the universe and know that there is something more. We can be both temporal and spiritual at once. Within this duality we try to live our lives as manifested between:

- Being free to choose, and being forced to live with choices made for us
- Being in control of life, and being controlled by outside forces
- Being useful, and feeling unnecessary
- Finding that life has meaning, and feeling that it is an empty nothingness

We did not choose to be born, we do not choose to die. Those choices are made elsewhere, by rules we cannot divine. Children begin with no choice, as a part of their mothers, and so must develop into being separate, gradually learning the skills of autonomy, with the ability to exercise choice.

As life proceeds towards its end, people slowly lose their choices, and watch their options slip away until there are none again. They need to find new peace as they watch their hard-earned gains disappear one by one. T.S. Eliot wrote:

We shall not cease from exploration
And the end of all our exploring
Will be to arrive where we started
And know the place for the first time.

We try to control our lives by most everything we do. We think we can acquire control if only we can have enough strength, power, money, beauty, admiration, knowledge, friends, guile, and lots of other things. Yet they never are enough.

We are not in control of life, and no matter how hard we try, the caprices of nature will win out over man. We can never predict what the outcome of an encounter will be. We can, however, exercise some control by participating in the process of our lives.

Even if our final destinies were decided by a table of random numbers somewhere in the universe, we would still be responsible for playing our roles, and well. So a Hindu prays to God to gain control of the body's breath, and heart, and pain. The Christian says, "God helps those who help themselves." Both recognize that we have a part in what our lives become, but the ultimate control remains with the forces of the universe.

We try to make ourselves useful so there is something left when we are gone. We seek to affect our personal destinies, those of others, and the destinies of those who are yet to come. We know that we must work, so we want to do things that "count" and make a difference. We want to be of value to ourselves and others.

There is little worse than feeling useless, and believing that it hardly matters that we were here at all. Is there a worse invective than being "worthless"? We work to avoid being insignificant, ineffective, and of no consequence. We want to find ways of being useful.

Amidst these ambiguities in choice, control, and usefulness, we look for the meaning of our lives and our place within the cosmos. We wonder at the purpose. Without meaning, we may as well be dead, for then there is only emptiness and despair. If we can comprehend that there is a meaning, in its service we can endure almost anything.

I thought I had lost everything. But I did have a glimmer of hope, for I was young and perhaps I would in time recover. In the future, I hoped, I might be able to pick up my old life again, the only life I knew. But that was never to happen, and any improvement was very slight. My body remained much the same.

Eventually, with time, a lot of help from others, and a lot of effort, I did slowly develop another kind of life. I was fortunate to find a way to put my medical degree to new use as a psychiatrist, and eventually returned to work, feeling useful in a new way. I met a lovely woman, and we made a life together. I rediscovered friendship, and found replacements for some of the things I used to do. It was a different life than the one before; nevertheless, it was a real one. I had regained some control over my life. I had choices once again, not those I had before, but very different ones, that nevertheless fulfilled my new life.

I loved, I worked, I traveled, I grew in unexpected

ways. My life, the new one, developed meaning for me once again, and I found some ways to reconcile it with the old one. I was, in short, alive.

But life is ever changing; and that is what makes it different from death. And, quite to my surprise, I am alive at sixty-four. I realize I have reached the autumn years of life, and soon the leaves must fall.

I am witness to my own decline. I watch one ability after another weaken and sometimes fail completely: writing, sitting, eating, breathing, bowel and bladder functions. I rarely even think of long-lost capacities now: to travel, to have a big night out, to play a sport. They are too remote.

My control over my life is gradually slipping away, my choices are fewer and fewer, my usefulness less and less. Those things that have given meaning to my life are in serious jeopardy.

I recently went through another bad period, when nothing in my body seemed to work. But this is not turning out as I expected it would. I really do not feel despair today. There is no particular reason for me to feel hope. Still, I am grateful for this day, and what it has brought me to.

I thought I would write of death, but instead I feel quite alive. In writing what I did of life and death, I seemed to reach another place, where I am pleased to be. Somehow, I do not fully understand, I feel freer from the troubles in my body, although they have not changed much.

What is this place of peace where no pain or worries wear me down? I know that feeling well and I know that it can appear at any time—to a considerable extent at least —regardless of how much my body aches. At times like this, I can look past my pain and incapacity. There is a lesson here I have to learn over and over again. How did I get here this time?

I was feeling very down and hopeless for quite a time. I had called a friend, just to hear his voice. We talked a bit of some insignificant things, but a word or two said by one of us, I cannot remember which, reminded me of my strength. The strength was that I had the choice to look past the gloom I felt to see the same simple objects in my life, and to look at them with fresh reverence, untarnished by my fears and doubts. Then I began to look toward them with the trust that they were just as they should be and nothing more.

Simply trying helped me to find the magic switch that changed the window of despair to one of hope. But to try, I had to be reminded that there was the choice to creatively face this day and that I have a commitment to make that choice. The stimulus was the conversation with my friend, yet the words we spoke were irrelevant, it seemed. It was, I think, that he was there to remind me of my strength and that I was not alone. This, more than anything that was said or done, had begun to open up alternatives to the place where I was stuck.

And today I saw my mother, who is still determined to live in her home alone. She seemed even more frail and slow and she tires very easily. I had thought her spirit was fading with her body. But as I looked at her today, I did not see the anguish I thought I had seen before—she seemed at peace and unafraid. I asked her if she had changed, or was it only I. She just smiled at me in reply.

I think I may be getting prepared to live, now that it is nearly time to die. What an unexpected transition this has now become. Perhaps in some amazing way, this life *is* a preparation, one whose work is done whenever it is over. Why else would I be getting better at it all the time?

Is this *the* great cosmic joke, the ultimate paradox that unmasks all human word and thought? Who but God could have such a wondrous sense of humor? Will I, then, be perfect when I die? Irony of all ironies.

ABOUT THE AUTHOR

ARNOLD R. BEISSER, M.D., is a clinical professor of psychiatry at the University of California at Los Angeles. A graduate of Stanford University and its medical school, he is also a Life Fellow of the American Psychiatric Association and a recipient of its Gold Achievement Award. He has published over one hundred articles, reviews, book chapters, and books, including *Madness in Sports, Mental Health Consultation*, and his recently acclaimed *Flying Without Wings*. He and his wife, Rita, live in Los Angeles.

BOOKMARK

The text of this book was set in twelve-point Bembo, with two points leading, by Berryville Digital Composition, of Berryville, Virginia. The display types are Centaur and Arrighi, composed by Zimmering Zinn & Madison, of New York. The book was printed and bound by Berryville Graphics. The typography and binding design are by Paul Randall Mize.